It's another Quality Book from CGP

This book is for 7-9 year olds —
it's ideal to use in class or with parents.

We've taken all those nasty terms from the Literacy Strategy, stuck them in a book — and made them easy.

Then we tried our little bests to make it funny — so you'll actually use it. Simple as that.

What CGP is all about

Our sole aim here at CGP is to produce the highest quality books — carefully written, immaculately presented, and dangerously close to being funny.

Then we work our socks off to get them out to you — at the cheapest possible prices.

Contents

Section Five — Kinds of Text

Section Six — Words About Writing

Section Seven — Poetry

Published by CGP
Typesetting, layout and illustrations by The English Coordination Group

Contributors:
Gemma Hallam
Kate Stevens
Claire Thompson

ISBN: 978 1 84146 151 9

Groovy website: www.cgpbooks.co.uk

Jolly bits of clipart from CorelDRAW®
Printed by Elanders Ltd, Newcastle upon Tyne.

Nouns

A noun is a word that names a thing, like a person, an animal or a place.

Or a vegetable!

Nouns name Things

1) Proper nouns are for particular things

Hello.
I'm Colin.

Proper nouns name a particular person, a particular place, a company or a team, a day of the week or a month of the year. They always begin with a capital letter.

Colin, India, Froggatt's Foods, Thursday, October

Don't forget — your name is a proper noun.
Always write people's names with a capital letter.

2) Common nouns are for kinds of thing

These are the common, everyday ones — as you'd expect. Common nouns name a kind of person or thing.

suitcase, hotdog, leaf, woman

3) Collective nouns are for groups of things

A collective noun is a word for a group of things.

bunch of flowers, herd of cows, flock of sheep

Common — as muck...

Nouns are words that name things. Nice and easy to start you off. The one tricky bit on this page is the rule about capital letters. Get this into your head — names of actual people, places, firms, sports teams, days and months ALL need a CAPITAL LETTER.

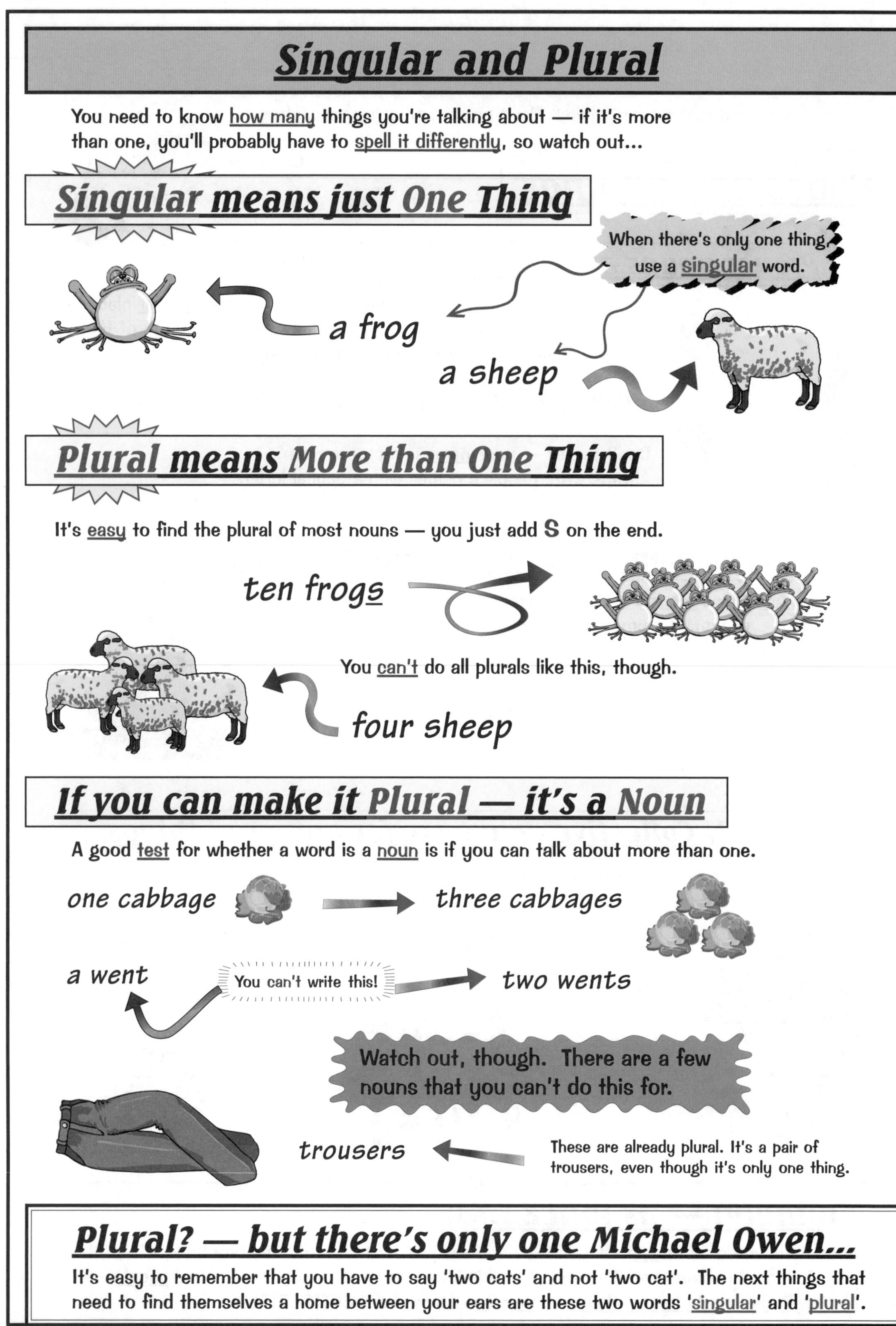

Singular and Plural

You need to know how many things you're talking about — if it's more than one, you'll probably have to spell it differently, so watch out...

Singular means just One Thing

When there's only one thing, use a singular word.

a frog

a sheep

Plural means More than One Thing

It's easy to find the plural of most nouns — you just add S on the end.

ten frogs

You can't do all plurals like this, though.

four sheep

If you can make it Plural — it's a Noun

A good test for whether a word is a noun is if you can talk about more than one.

one cabbage → three cabbages

a went → two wents

You can't write this!

Watch out, though. There are a few nouns that you can't do this for.

trousers

These are already plural. It's a pair of trousers, even though it's only one thing.

Plural? — but there's only one Michael Owen...

It's easy to remember that you have to say 'two cats' and not 'two cat'. The next things that need to find themselves a home between your ears are these two words 'singular' and 'plural'.

Verbs

You need to know what verbs are and how to use them properly, so read on.

A Verb is a Doing word

Doing words are verbs — they're words about doing an action. Verbs tell you what's going on in the sentence. A sentence has to have a verb in it for it to make sense.

Carl likes disco music.

the verb is 'likes'

Being words are verbs too:

Shirley is happy.

the verb is 'is'

Verb Agreement is getting your Verbs Right

When the verb and the noun doing the action go together, then they agree.
If they don't go together, the sentence won't make sense.

John has buried his dad in the sand.

'Has buried' goes with John.

You can't write 'John have buried'!

The Tense of a verb is Past, Present or Future

The tense of a verb tells you when the action is happening.
Verbs can be in the past tense, the present tense or the future tense.

Roberta fought for the rights of vegetables. — past

Roberta fights for the rights of vegetables. — present

Roberta will fight for the rights of vegetables. — future

Verbs tense? — take some deep breaths...

There it is, then — a verb is an action word or a being word. No sentence would dream of being seen without one. Don't stuff a verb in any old how — you've got to make it go with the noun that's doing it. In other words, don't write "you is" or "they wants" or anything daft like that.

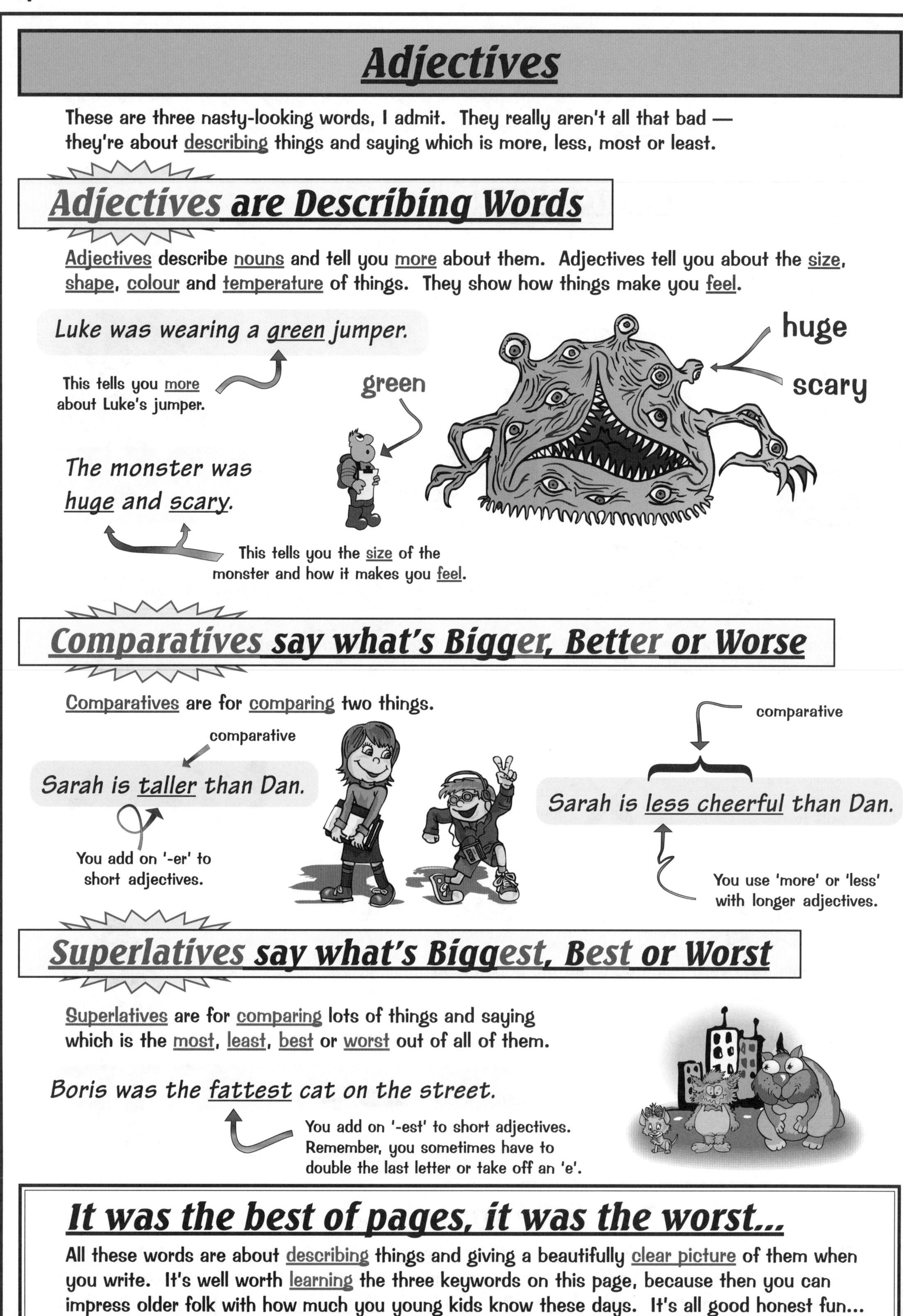

Adjectives

These are three nasty-looking words, I admit. They really aren't all that bad — they're about describing things and saying which is more, less, most or least.

Adjectives are Describing Words

Adjectives describe nouns and tell you more about them. Adjectives tell you about the size, shape, colour and temperature of things. They show how things make you feel.

Luke was wearing a green jumper.

This tells you more about Luke's jumper.

The monster was huge and scary.

This tells you the size of the monster and how it makes you feel.

Comparatives say what's Bigger, Better or Worse

Comparatives are for comparing two things.

Sarah is taller than Dan.

You add on '-er' to short adjectives.

Sarah is less cheerful than Dan.

You use 'more' or 'less' with longer adjectives.

Superlatives say what's Biggest, Best or Worst

Superlatives are for comparing lots of things and saying which is the most, least, best or worst out of all of them.

Boris was the fattest cat on the street.

You add on '-est' to short adjectives. Remember, you sometimes have to double the last letter or take off an 'e'.

It was the best of pages, it was the worst...

All these words are about describing things and giving a beautifully clear picture of them when you write. It's well worth learning the three keywords on this page, because then you can impress older folk with how much you young kids know these days. It's all good honest fun...

Adverbs

Adverbs are the '-ly' words that say how something was done. They're very useful for describing what happens in stories and poems and making your writing more interesting.

Adverbs describe Verbs

Adverbs describe verbs. They tell you more about how the action was done. Adverbs end in -ly. Adverbs don't have to be one word — they can be a group of words.

Adverbs describe Adjectives

Words like 'totally', 'quite' and 'very' are adverbs. They're used with adjectives to show how much the adjective is working on the noun.

a happy dog

a very happy dog

Adverbs — they add to verbs...

Adverbs are words that tell you more about a verb or an adjective. It's easy to remember the word if you think of it as something that 'adds' to verbs. You've got to remember they add to adjectives too — that's more tricky, so get it firmly stuck between your ears now.

Little Words

Sentences have these tinsy little short words as well as nouns, verbs and adjectives. They do lots of different jobs in the sentence. Learn what they're called and what they're for.

Pronouns do the job of Nouns

Pronouns stand in for nouns in a sentence to stop you repeating yourself too much.

Tanya asked some tortoises to tea.
Tanya gave the tortoises tea and chocolate biscuits.

Bo-ring.

This is much better because it doesn't keep repeating the same words.

Tanya asked some tortoises to tea.
She gave them tea and chocolate biscuits.

'She' stands in for the name Tanya. It's still about her, but it doesn't use her name.

The tortoises are 'them'. You can't write 'gave they'.

Conjunctions join bits of a Sentence Together

Conjunctions are words like 'and', 'but' and 'then'. They join words together in a sentence. They also join two short sentences together to make one long one.

Iqbal and Tina got up on stage. They sang together.

'And' joins the two words together here.

Iqbal and Tina got up on stage and sang together.

'And' joins the two bits of the sentence together here.

...but wait, there's more! So, if, while, when, however, because, and though are all conjunctions too.

Little words in sentences — sent, ten, set...

It's easy to forget about the little words in a sentence. They're all important though, so you'd better make sure you know about them — read this page until it's firmly lodged in your bonce.

Sentences

The thing about a sentence is that it's got to make sense. If you read it and think "Eh? what's going on there, then?", chances are it's not a proper sentence.

Sentences make Sense on their Own

A sentence can only make sense if it's about something. It can only be about something happening if it's got a verb — that's a good rule to remember. A sentence begins with a capital letter and ends with a full stop, a question mark or an exclamation mark.

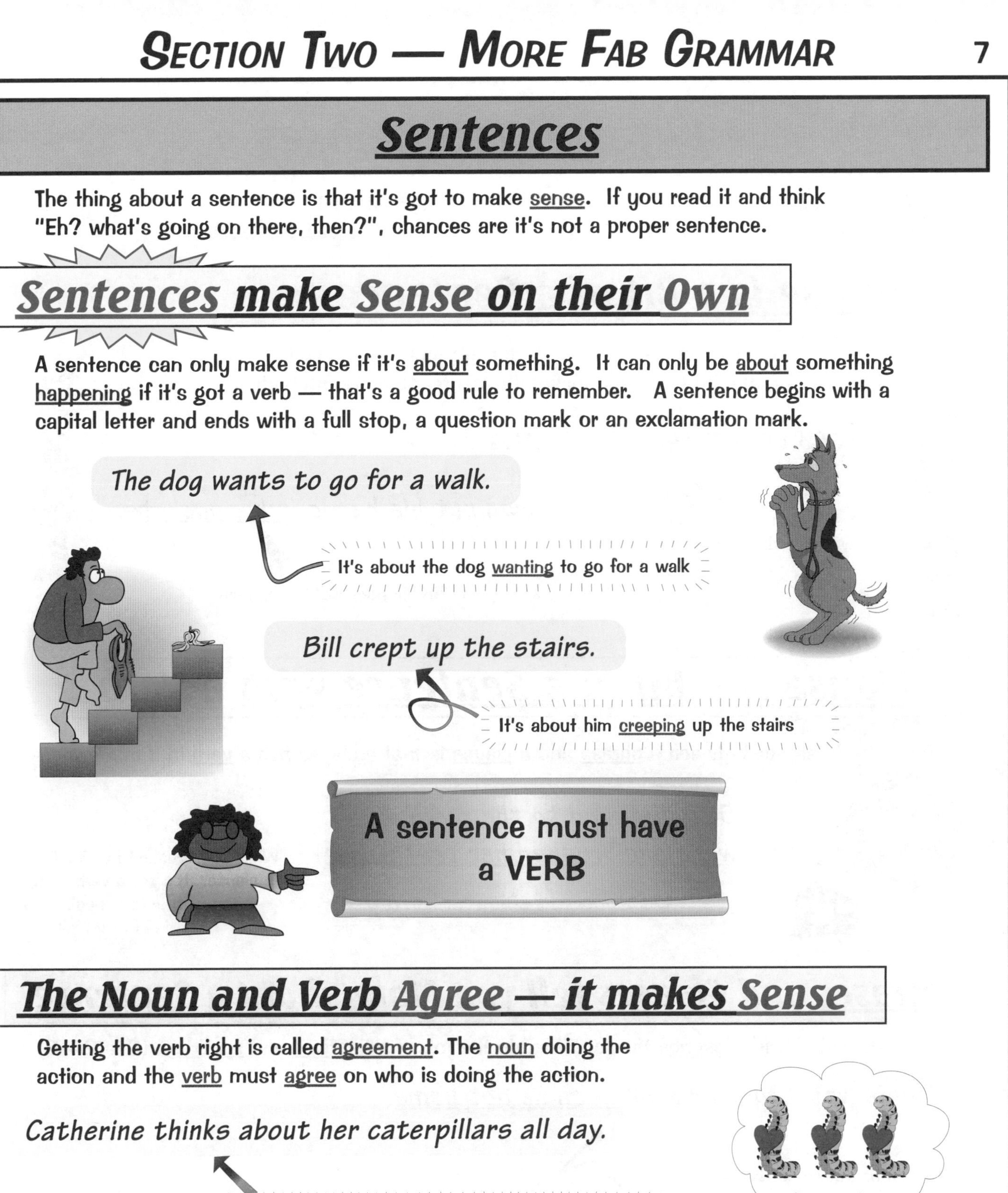

The dog wants to go for a walk.

It's about the dog wanting to go for a walk

Bill crept up the stairs.

It's about him creeping up the stairs

A sentence must have a VERB

The Noun and Verb Agree — it makes Sense

Getting the verb right is called agreement. The noun doing the action and the verb must agree on who is doing the action.

Catherine thinks about her caterpillars all day.

Catherine is doing the action — the verb is 'thinks'.

The caterpillars think about Catherine.

The caterpillars are doing the action — the verb is 'think'.

Say it out loud — that's a verb-al agreement

Knowing that sentences have to make sense on their own is more useful than knowing that they begin with a capital letter and end with a full stop. Agreement is just a funny old way of saying that if you don't get your verb right, your sentence will look wrong and it won't make sense.

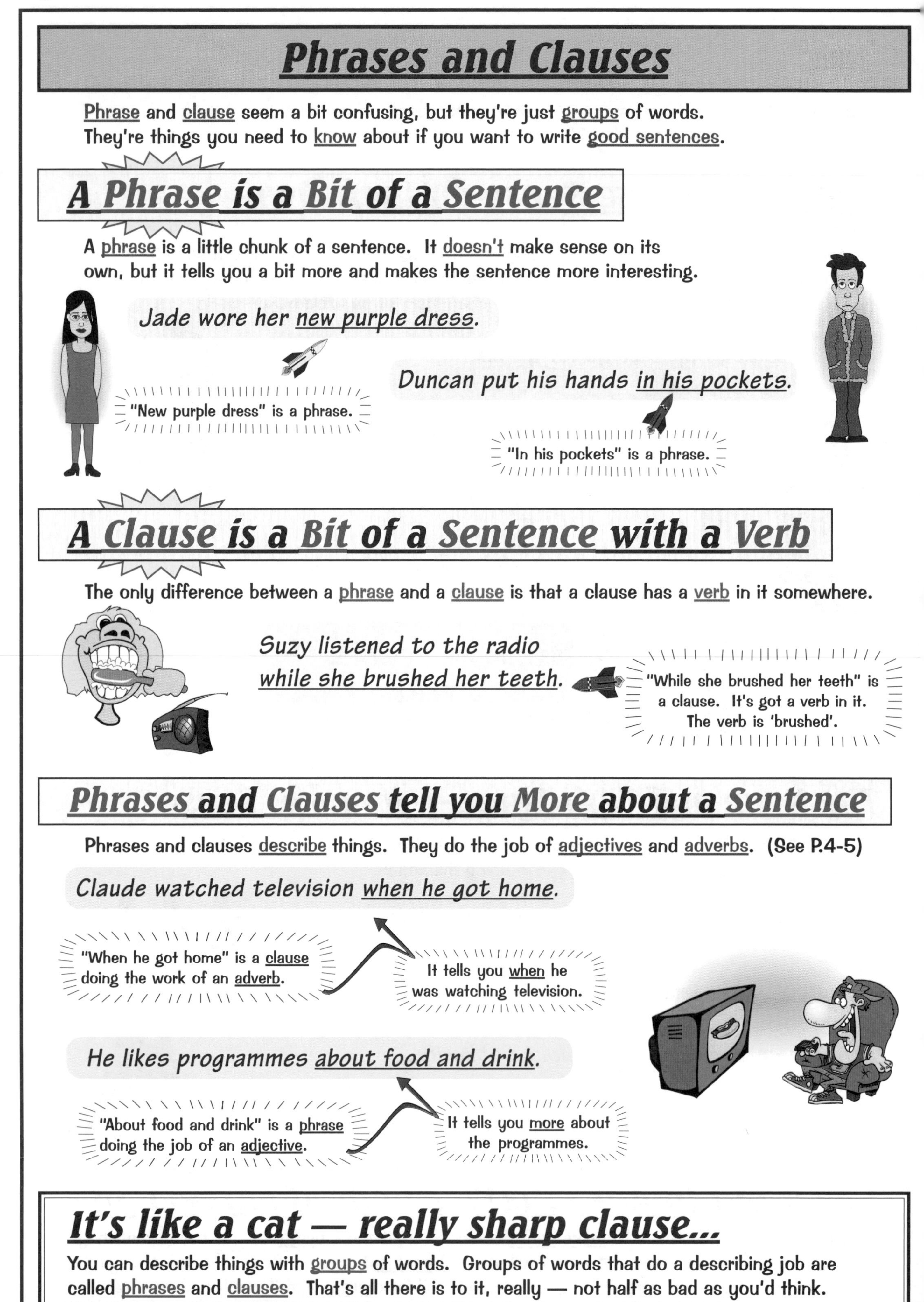

Phrases and Clauses

Phrase and clause seem a bit confusing, but they're just groups of words. They're things you need to know about if you want to write good sentences.

A Phrase is a Bit of a Sentence

A phrase is a little chunk of a sentence. It doesn't make sense on its own, but it tells you a bit more and makes the sentence more interesting.

Jade wore her new purple dress.

"New purple dress" is a phrase.

Duncan put his hands in his pockets.

"In his pockets" is a phrase.

A Clause is a Bit of a Sentence with a Verb

The only difference between a phrase and a clause is that a clause has a verb in it somewhere.

Suzy listened to the radio while she brushed her teeth.

"While she brushed her teeth" is a clause. It's got a verb in it. The verb is 'brushed'.

Phrases and Clauses tell you More about a Sentence

Phrases and clauses describe things. They do the job of adjectives and adverbs. (See P.4-5)

Claude watched television when he got home.

"When he got home" is a clause doing the work of an adverb.

It tells you when he was watching television.

He likes programmes about food and drink.

"About food and drink" is a phrase doing the job of an adjective.

It tells you more about the programmes.

It's like a cat — really sharp clause...

You can describe things with groups of words. Groups of words that do a describing job are called phrases and clauses. That's all there is to it, really — not half as bad as you'd think.

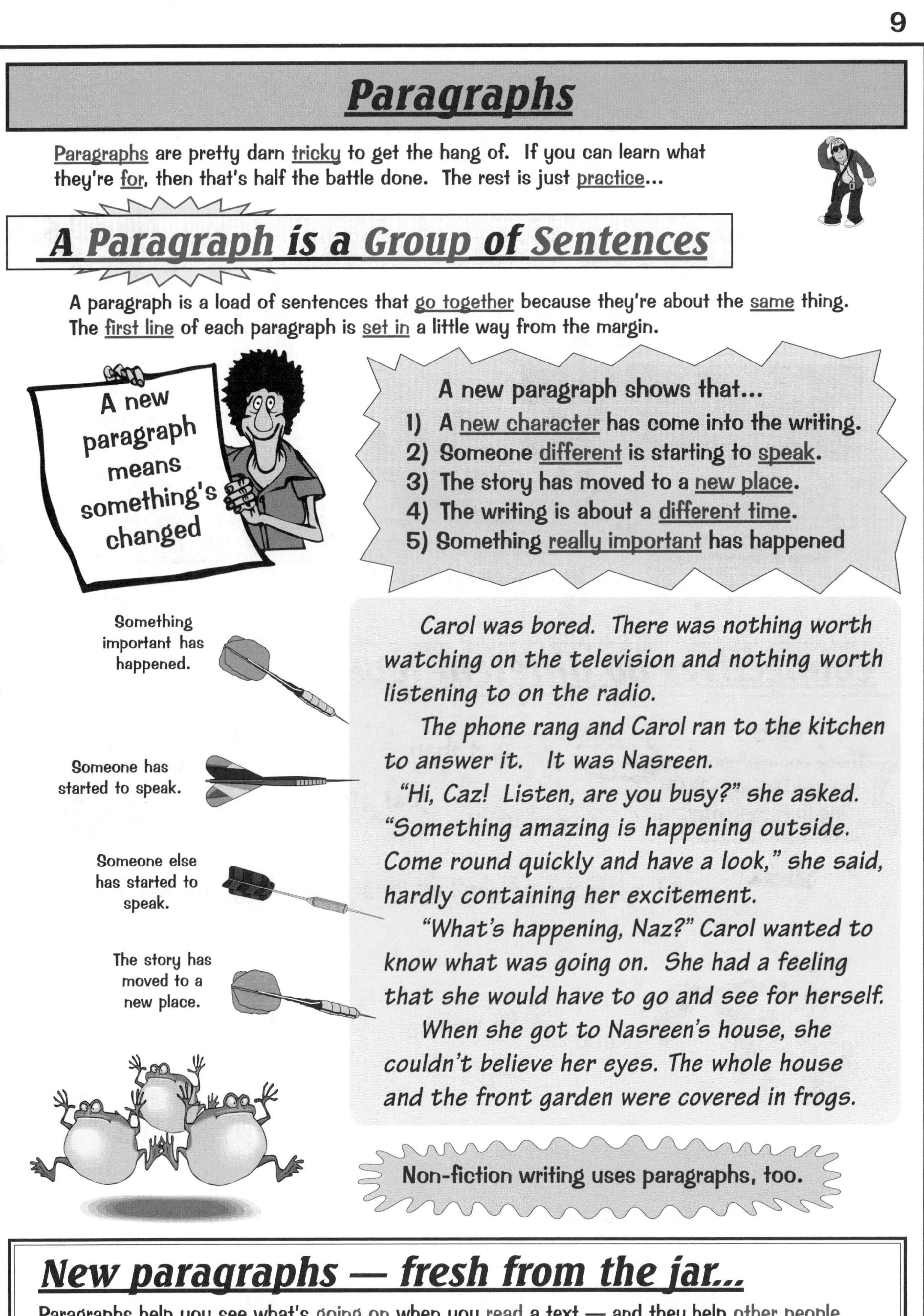

Paragraphs

Paragraphs are pretty darn tricky to get the hang of. If you can learn what they're for, then that's half the battle done. The rest is just practice...

A Paragraph is a Group of Sentences

A paragraph is a load of sentences that go together because they're about the same thing. The first line of each paragraph is set in a little way from the margin.

A new paragraph shows that...

1) A new character has come into the writing.
2) Someone different is starting to speak.
3) The story has moved to a new place.
4) The writing is about a different time.
5) Something really important has happened

Carol was bored. There was nothing worth watching on the television and nothing worth listening to on the radio.

The phone rang and Carol ran to the kitchen to answer it. It was Nasreen.

"Hi, Caz! Listen, are you busy?" she asked. "Something amazing is happening outside. Come round quickly and have a look," she said, hardly containing her excitement.

"What's happening, Naz?" Carol wanted to know what was going on. She had a feeling that she would have to go and see for herself.

When she got to Nasreen's house, she couldn't believe her eyes. The whole house and the front garden were covered in frogs.

Non-fiction writing uses paragraphs, too.

New paragraphs — fresh from the jar...

Paragraphs help you see what's going on when you read a text — and they help other people read what you've written. Now you know all about paragraphs there's no excuse not to use them. If you do it will change your life — your writing will be a million times better, anyway...

Connectives

If you know about these pesky little things, you'll see how sentences join together and then you can start writing bigger, better, beefier sentences yourself.

Connectives Join Parts of a Text

Connectives join clauses together, they link one sentence up with the next, or they start off a new paragraph.

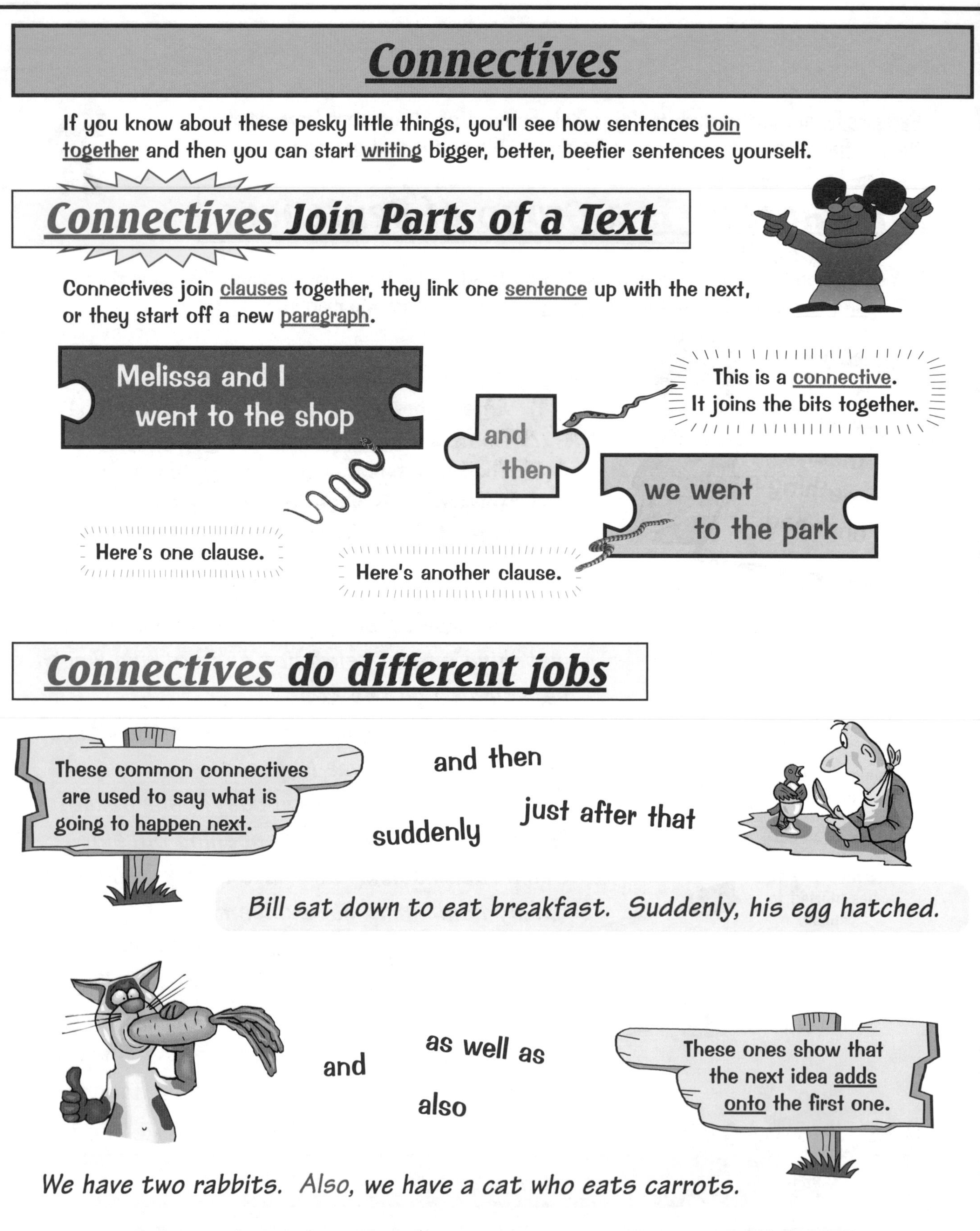

Connectives do different jobs

These common connectives are used to say what is going to happen next.

and then

suddenly

just after that

Bill sat down to eat breakfast. Suddenly, his egg hatched.

and

as well as

also

These ones show that the next idea adds onto the first one.

We have two rabbits. Also, we have a cat who eats carrots.

Kirsten had chocolate sauce as well as ketchup on her chips

Disconnected — dial 100 for the operator...

They're just like glue — connectives stick sentences, clauses and paragraphs together. Make sure you learn a few so you can make lovely long sentences yourself and life will be much rosier...

Punctuation

You know what punctuation is — you've just got to make sure you use it. All the time. Here's the blindingly important stuff you should never forget when you write a sentence.

Start with a Capital Letter

He started to panic.

The ants were here to stay.

Use a capital letter at the start of every sentence.

A Full Stop goes at the end

It's the easiest thing in the world to forget.

Your sentence isn't finished until you've put in the full stop.

FINISH

full stop

It's as simple as that.

Exclamation and Question Marks end sentences too

You use an exclamation mark to show really strong feelings.

"Ouch, that was my foot!"

"Don't jump, Mark!"

You don't need a full stop as well — only the exclamation mark.

You use a question mark if the sentence is a question. Easy.

Where did Lucas leave his cookies?

Remember — no full stop here.

Punctuation — it's a life sentence...

This is straight-down-the-middle kind of stuff, I'd say. It doesn't hurt to get the basics right, though, so test yourself on each heading to make sure you really know it. Easy peasy.

Commas

Commas are easy to put in, but tricky to get right. Learn this stuff.

Commas are used in Lists

You've done this before, but it's worth remembering.
A comma goes after every word in the list except the last one.
Then 'and' or an 'or' goes between the last two words.

The foxes wore trainers, ties, hats and sunglasses.

Commas mean there's something New Coming

If you've got two different ideas in your head when you think of your sentence, you need a comma in between them.

The squirrel pounced, frightening the giraffe.

Comma thieves — in for a long sentence...

Two big juicy things about commas here, then — now get them learned. Commas in lists are pretty easy. Just don't forget that a comma also goes between two ideas in a sentence.

Speech Marks

Speech marks are the two pairs of little squiggles we put around text to show when somebody is talking.

Speech Marks show when Someone is Speaking

Speech marks go before and after the words which are spoken:

Speech marks open the actual speech.

Speech marks close it again.

"A little bit of custard never hurt anyone," Agnes said.

The first spoken word always has a capital letter.

Burt asked, "Do you think the pizza is ready?"

Capital letter

When People Speak you start a New Paragraph

Every time someone starts speaking, you start a new paragraph.

New paragraph every time someone new speaks.

The giraffe ran into the room and hid behind Peter.

"What's the matter?" Peter asked the quivering creature.

"The squirrel is after me again," the giraffe sobbed. "Don't let it get me!"

Don't need a new paragraph here because it's the same person talking.

Speech marks — the Queen gets 10 out of 10...

Put speech marks when someone starts to speak, and then when they finish and Bob's your uncle. Make sure you always start a new paragraph when someone new speaks — and don't forget those all-important capital letters for the first spoken word. Get it into your head and keep it there.

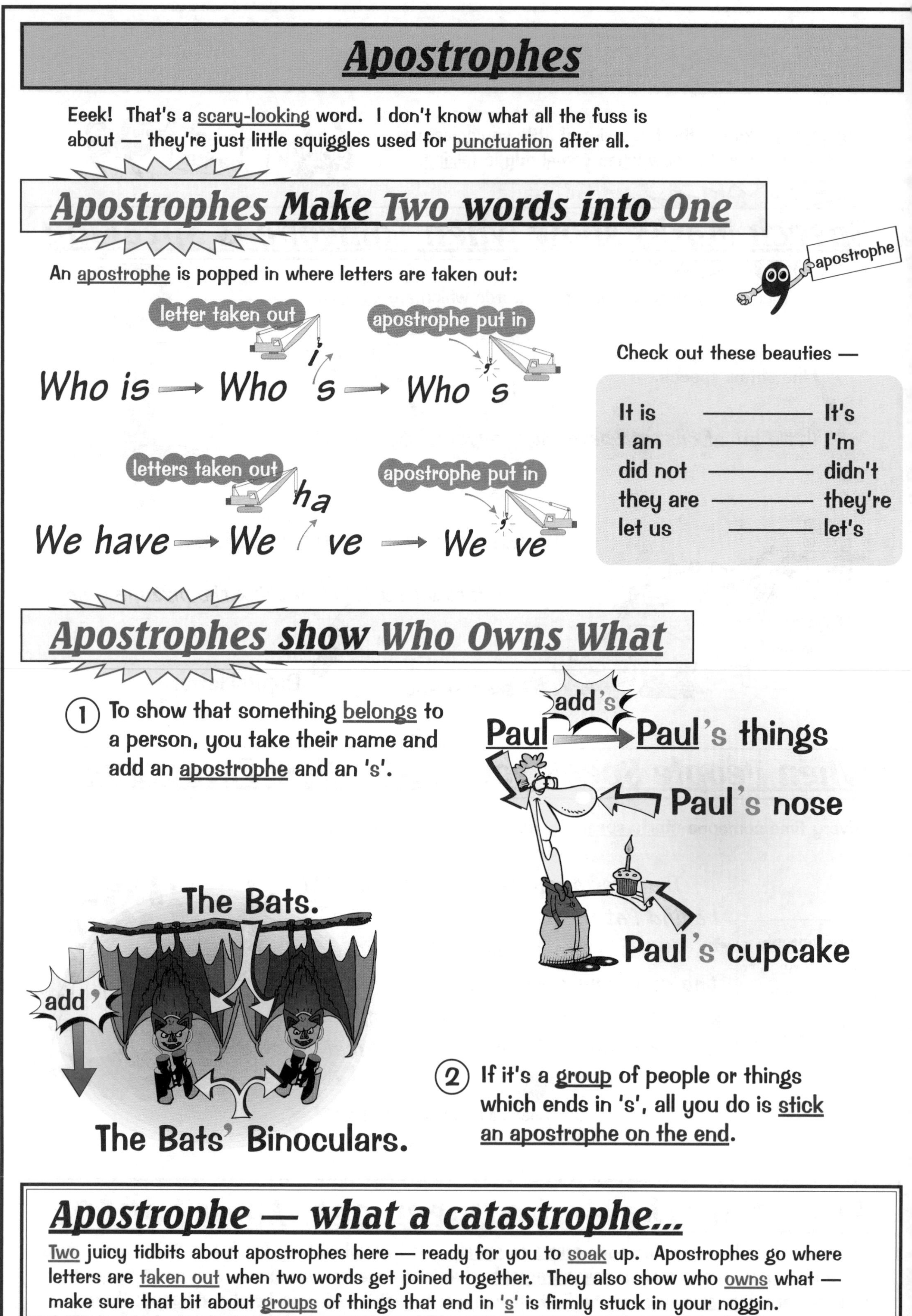

Apostrophes

Eeek! That's a scary-looking word. I don't know what all the fuss is about — they're just little squiggles used for punctuation after all.

Apostrophes Make Two words into One

An apostrophe is popped in where letters are taken out:

Check out these beauties —

It is	It's
I am	I'm
did not	didn't
they are	they're
let us	let's

Apostrophes show Who Owns What

1. To show that something belongs to a person, you take their name and add an apostrophe and an 's'.

2. If it's a group of people or things which ends in 's', all you do is stick an apostrophe on the end.

Apostrophe — what a catastrophe...

Two juicy tidbits about apostrophes here — ready for you to soak up. Apostrophes go where letters are taken out when two words get joined together. They also show who owns what — make sure that bit about groups of things that end in 's' is firmly stuck in your noggin.

More Punctuation

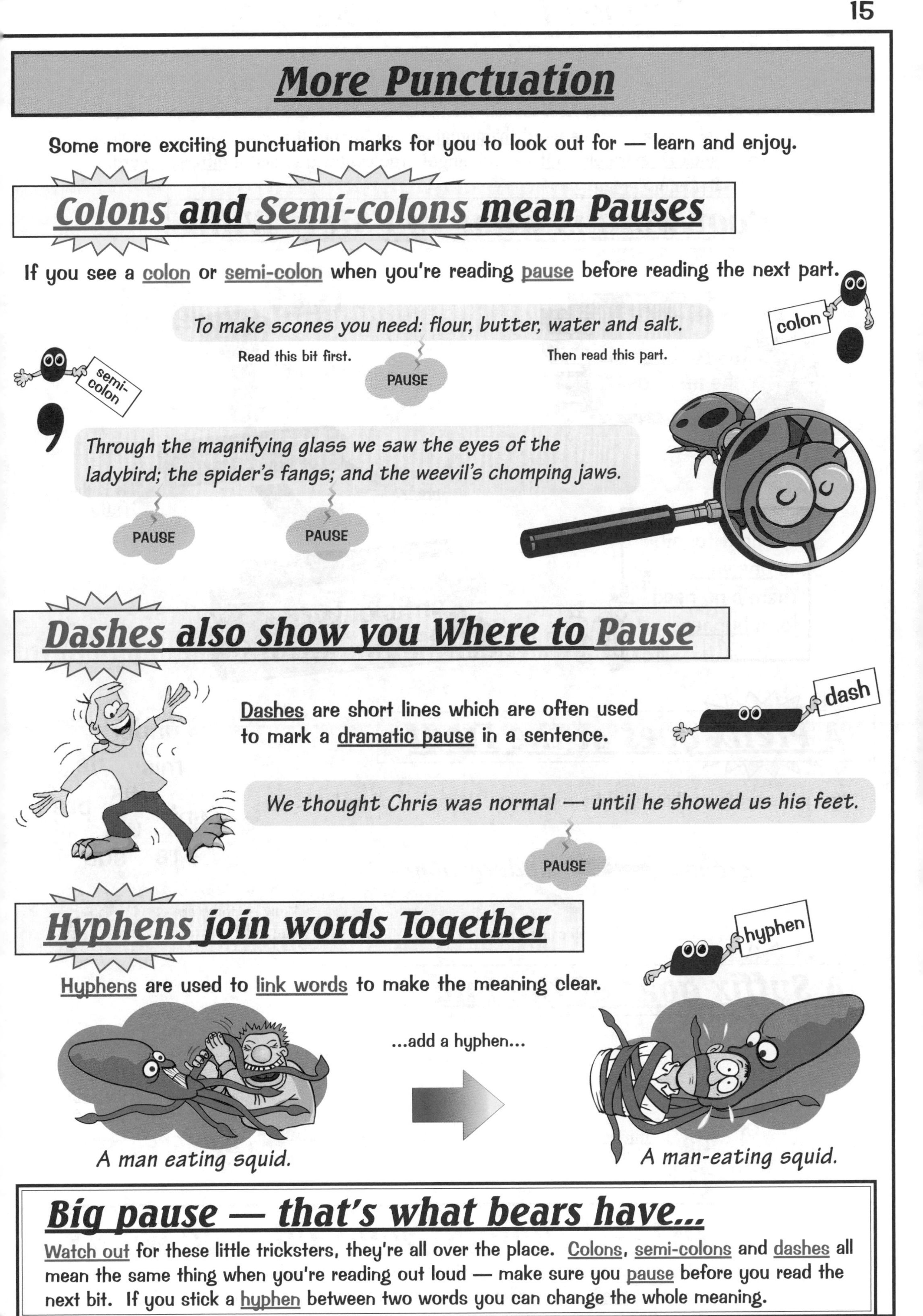

Some more exciting punctuation marks for you to look out for — learn and enjoy.

Colons and Semi-colons mean Pauses

If you see a colon or semi-colon when you're reading pause before reading the next part.

To make scones you need: flour, butter, water and salt.

Read this bit first. PAUSE Then read this part.

Through the magnifying glass we saw the eyes of the ladybird; the spider's fangs; and the weevil's chomping jaws.

PAUSE PAUSE

Dashes also show you Where to Pause

Dashes are short lines which are often used to mark a dramatic pause in a sentence.

We thought Chris was normal — until he showed us his feet.

PAUSE

Hyphens join words Together

Hyphens are used to link words to make the meaning clear.

A man eating squid.

...add a hyphen...

A man-eating squid.

Big pause — that's what bears have...

Watch out for these little tricksters, they're all over the place. Colons, semi-colons and dashes all mean the same thing when you're reading out loud — make sure you pause before you read the next bit. If you stick a hyphen between two words you can change the whole meaning.

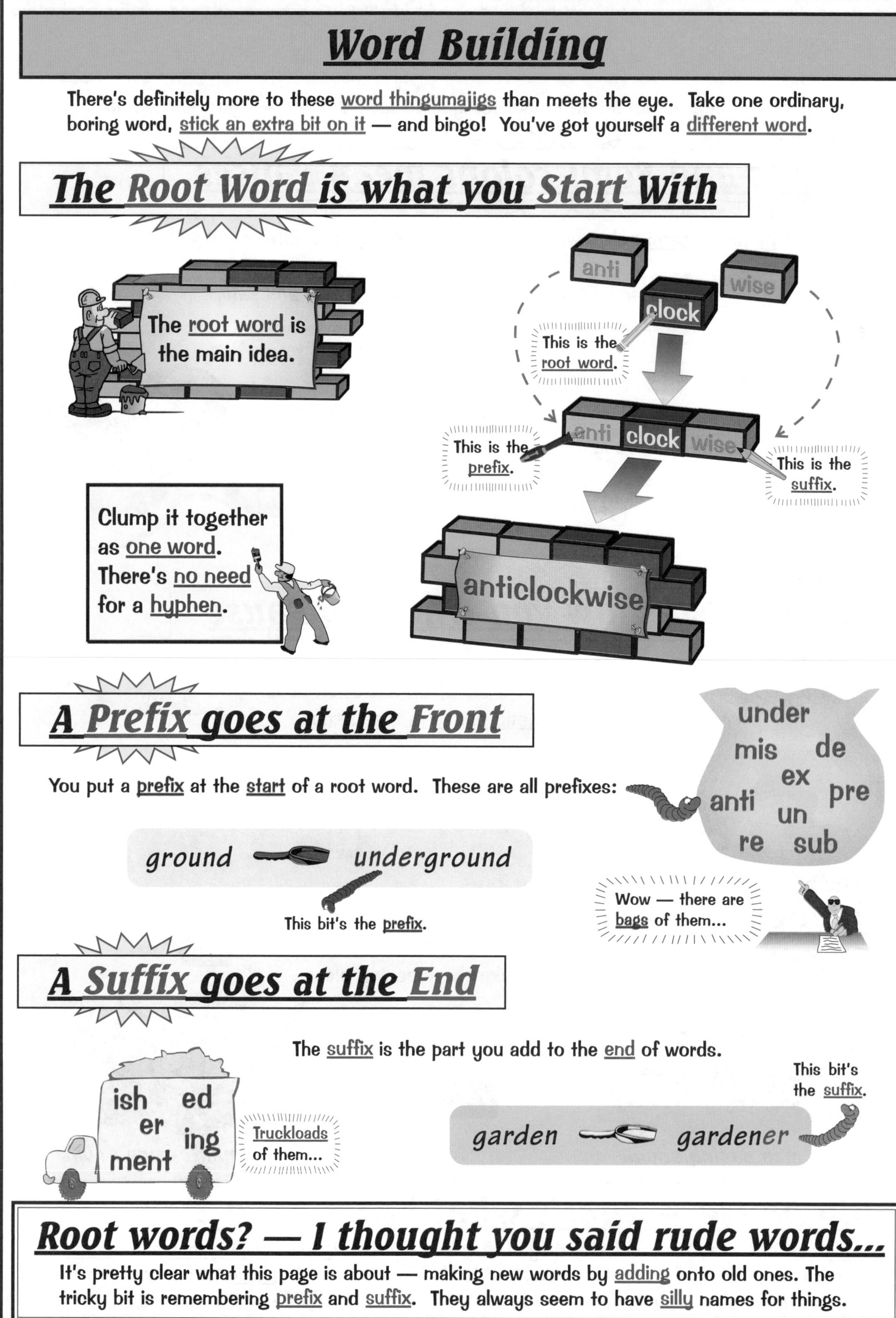

Word Building

There's definitely more to these word thingumajigs than meets the eye. Take one ordinary, boring word, stick an extra bit on it — and bingo! You've got yourself a different word.

The Root Word is what you Start With

A Prefix goes at the Front

You put a prefix at the start of a root word. These are all prefixes:

A Suffix goes at the End

The suffix is the part you add to the end of words.

Root words? — I thought you said rude words...

It's pretty clear what this page is about — making new words by adding onto old ones. The tricky bit is remembering prefix and suffix. They always seem to have silly names for things.

Same, Opposite and Mini

It's amazing how they can come up with such big words to talk about simple things.
Here are three of them — don't let their names put you off, just go and learn them.

Synonyms are words that Mean the Same

Words like "big" and "large" are synonyms — they mean the same thing.
Synonym is bit of a daft name, but that's what they're called, so you're stuck with it.

These are synonyms for the word scared...

frightened, petrified, terrified

Sarah was scared. She was wearing Arthur's kennel again and she knew he'd be cross.

angry, furious, annoyed

... and these are synonyms for the word "cross".

Antonyms are Opposites

Opposite words are things like "hot" and "cold" — and they're called antonyms.
You can use some prefixes and suffixes to make antonyms:

Prefixes like these make opposites:

anti un mis dis in non

happy → unhappy

Add ful and less to a root word and you get two opposite words.

care → careful
care → careless

Diminutives Shrink Things

Diminutives are words that make things sound small. You could add a suffix like kin, let or y on the end of a word...

pig → piglet

Jane → Janey

...or put another word before it, like little.

little Jane

Help me — I think I'm shrinking...

Don't get antonyms and synonyms muddled up — remember: synonym = same. Diminutive is a silly big word for a simple thing — you just use them to make things sound small.

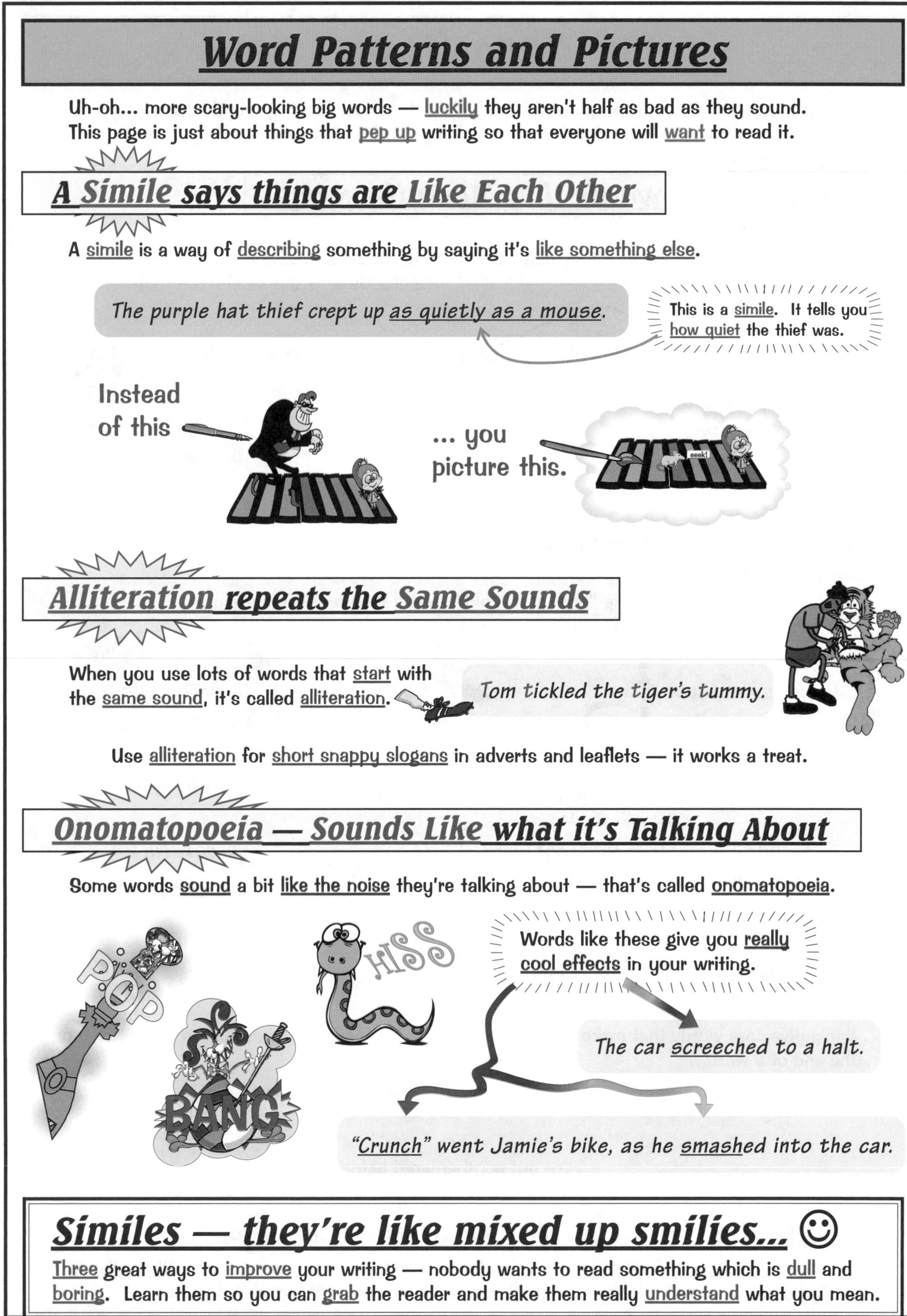

Word Patterns and Pictures

Uh-oh... more scary-looking big words — luckily they aren't half as bad as they sound. This page is just about things that pep up writing so that everyone will want to read it.

A Simile says things are Like Each Other

A simile is a way of describing something by saying it's like something else.

The purple hat thief crept up as quietly as a mouse.

This is a simile. It tells you how quiet the thief was.

Instead of this ... you picture this.

Alliteration repeats the Same Sounds

When you use lots of words that start with the same sound, it's called alliteration.

Tom tickled the tiger's tummy.

Use alliteration for short snappy slogans in adverts and leaflets — it works a treat.

Onomatopoeia — Sounds Like what it's Talking About

Some words sound a bit like the noise they're talking about — that's called onomatopoeia.

Words like these give you really cool effects in your writing.

The car screeched to a halt.

"Crunch" went Jamie's bike, as he smashed into the car.

Similes — they're like mixed up smilies... ☺

Three great ways to improve your writing — nobody wants to read something which is dull and boring. Learn them so you can grab the reader and make them really understand what you mean.

Homophones and Puns

Spelling gets a bit tricky when words sound the same as each other, so you'd better watch out. On the other hand, you wouldn't be able to make all those side-splitting puns without them...

Homophones are words which Sound the Same

Homophones are words that mean different things, but sound the same.

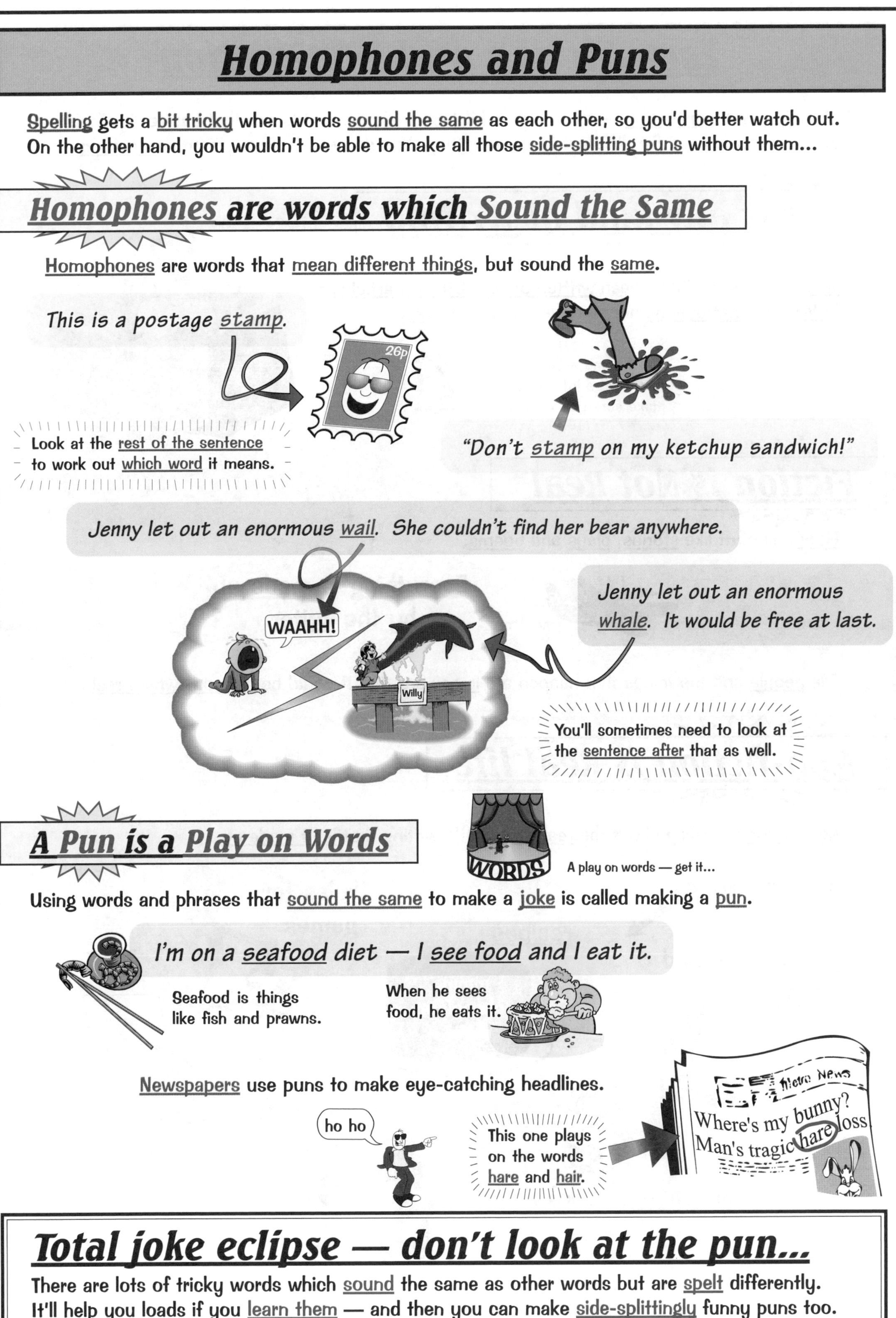

A Pun is a Play on Words

Using words and phrases that sound the same to make a joke is called making a pun.

Newspapers use puns to make eye-catching headlines.

Total joke eclipse — don't look at the pun...

There are lots of tricky words which sound the same as other words but are spelt differently. It'll help you loads if you learn them — and then you can make side-splittingly funny puns too.

Fact, Fiction and Non-Fiction

Text, fiction and non-fiction — all sounds a bit technical to me. It's not that bad really, they're just fancy words used for different kinds of writing. You do need to know them, so read on.

Text is any kind of Writing

Text means stuff that's been written down. Stories, articles, letters and instructions are all different kinds of text.

Fiction is Not Real

Fiction is stuff like stories, plays and poems.

The people and the things that happen are imaginary, but it could be set somewhere real.

Non-fiction is Real life

Non-fiction is writing about the real world. It's writing that isn't made up.

That's things like:

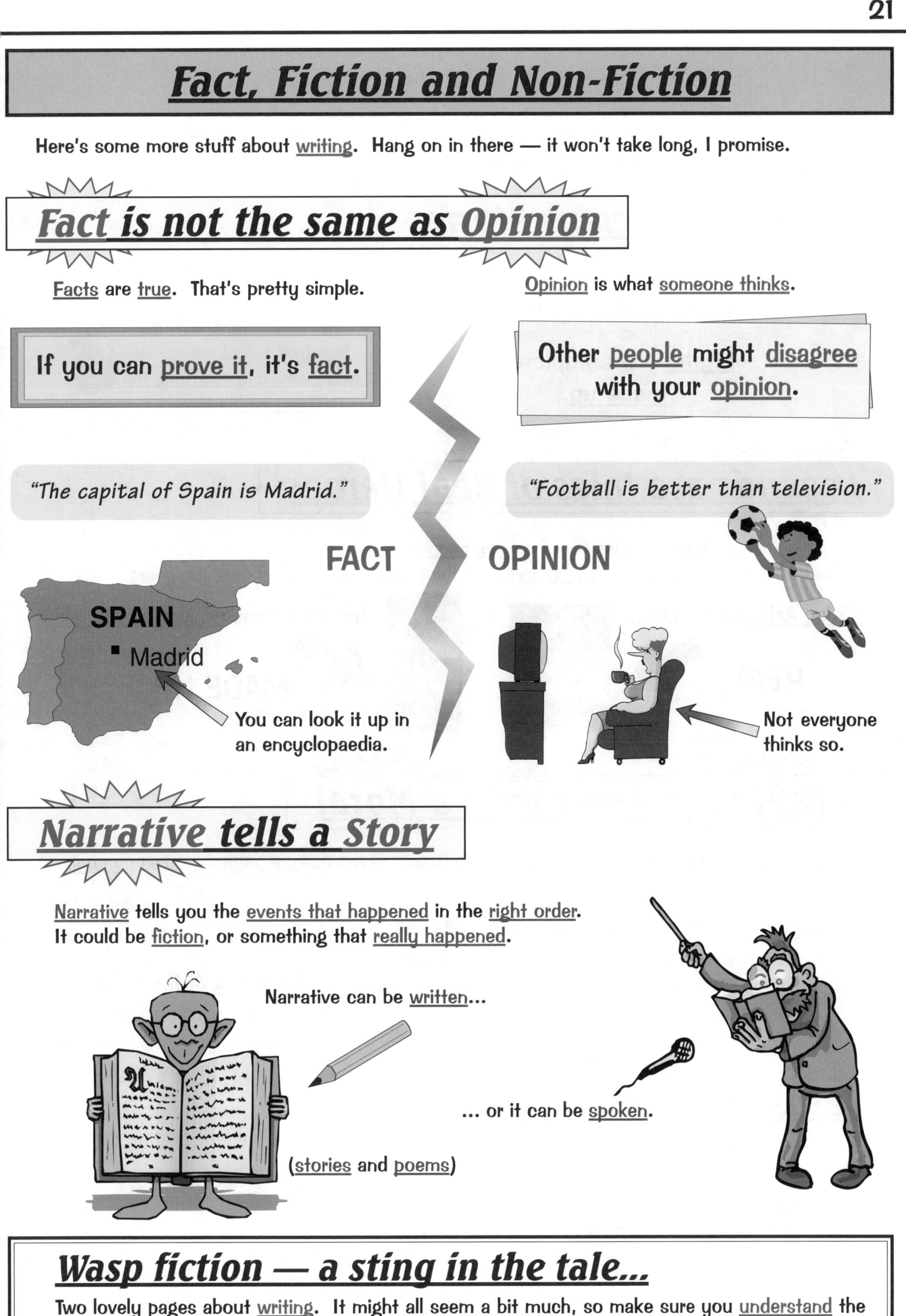

Fact, Fiction and Non-Fiction

Here's some more stuff about writing. Hang on in there — it won't take long, I promise.

Fact is not the same as Opinion

Facts are true. That's pretty simple.

If you can prove it, it's fact.

"The capital of Spain is Madrid."

Opinion is what someone thinks.

Other people might disagree with your opinion.

"Football is better than television."

You can look it up in an encyclopaedia.

Not everyone thinks so.

Narrative tells a Story

Narrative tells you the events that happened in the right order.
It could be fiction, or something that really happened.

Narrative can be written...

(stories and poems)

... or it can be spoken.

Wasp fiction — a sting in the tale...

Two lovely pages about writing. It might all seem a bit much, so make sure you understand the information under each heading before you go onto the next one — it's not that bad really.

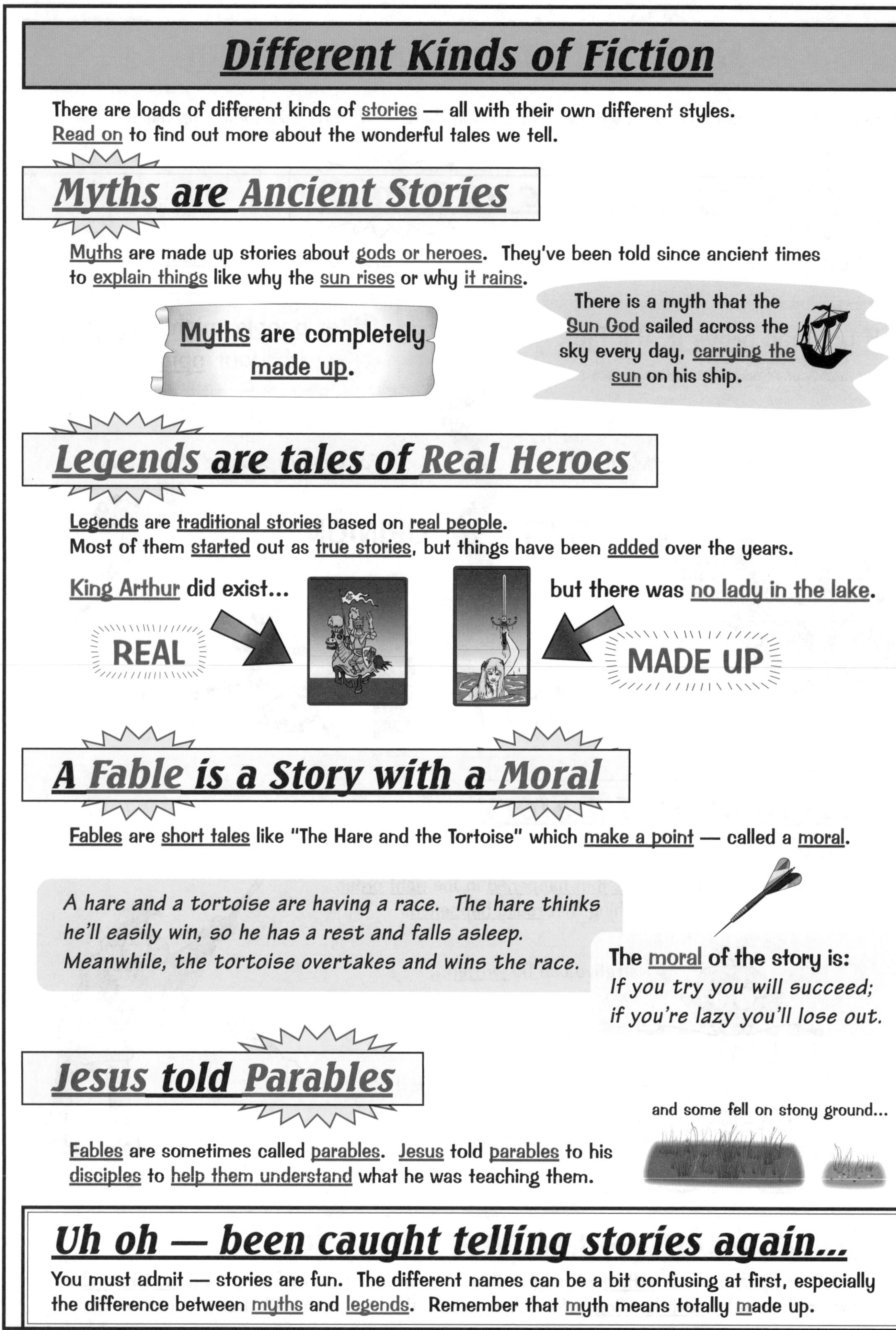

Different Kinds of Fiction

There are loads of different kinds of stories — all with their own different styles.
Read on to find out more about the wonderful tales we tell.

Myths are Ancient Stories

Myths are made up stories about gods or heroes. They've been told since ancient times to explain things like why the sun rises or why it rains.

Myths are completely made up.

There is a myth that the Sun God sailed across the sky every day, carrying the sun on his ship.

Legends are tales of Real Heroes

Legends are traditional stories based on real people.
Most of them started out as true stories, but things have been added over the years.

King Arthur did exist... but there was no lady in the lake.

A Fable is a Story with a Moral

Fables are short tales like "The Hare and the Tortoise" which make a point — called a moral.

A hare and a tortoise are having a race. The hare thinks he'll easily win, so he has a rest and falls asleep. Meanwhile, the tortoise overtakes and wins the race.

The moral of the story is:
If you try you will succeed; if you're lazy you'll lose out.

Jesus told Parables

Fables are sometimes called parables. Jesus told parables to his disciples to help them understand what he was teaching them.

Uh oh — been caught telling stories again...

You must admit — stories are fun. The different names can be a bit confusing at first, especially the difference between myths and legends. Remember that myth means totally made up.

Different Kinds of Fiction

Stories are not boring — no way. They can be about all sorts of weird and wonderful things. Here are three kinds of story you're bound to have come across.

Fairy Tales are Children's Stories

Fairy tales are stories written for children. There are hundreds of them, but you can spot the same ideas in all of them:

1) good defeating evil,
2) a happy ending.

Hansel and Gretel, Rapunzel... you've heard them all before.

Fantasy Adventures are Magical

Fantasy adventures are stories where magic happens. You could be in an imaginary world with witches and elves... or you could be somewhere totally ordinary, but with really weird things happening.
In other words...

if your teacher turns into a fire-breathing hamster in the middle of a Maths lesson...

1+2 = 3

... or you're sitting in a magic tree with a pixie,

— it's a fantasy story.

Science fiction is usually Set in the Future

Science fiction stories are about space, aliens or time travel. Just think of things like Star Wars and Star Trek.

They're often set in the future.

A long time ago, in a galaxy far, far away...

Stories can be about all sorts of things — just take a look in your library. I bet you've read stories like these before, now you just need to learn all the nitty gritty details.

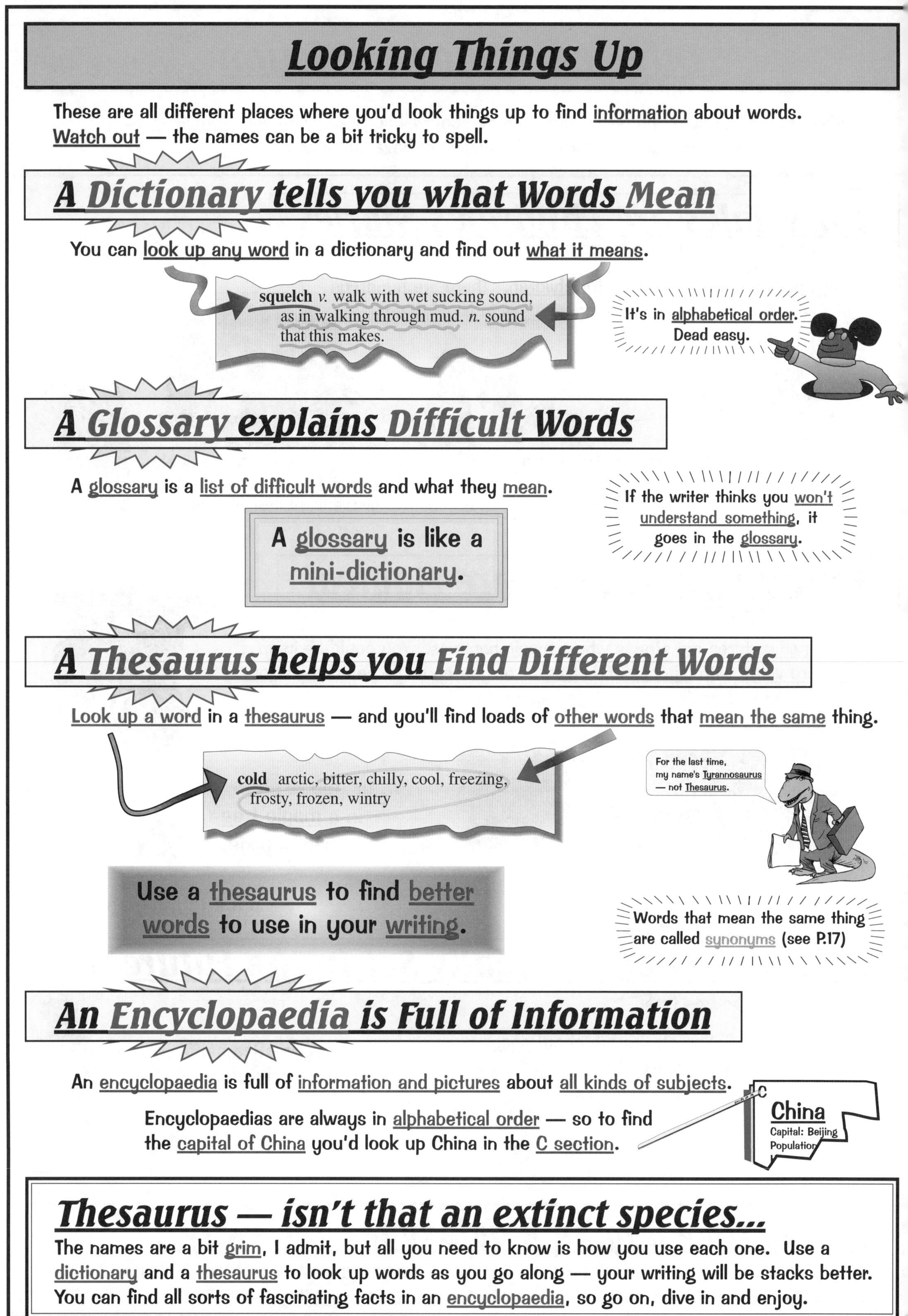

Looking Things Up

These are all different places where you'd look things up to find information about words. Watch out — the names can be a bit tricky to spell.

A Dictionary tells you what Words Mean

You can look up any word in a dictionary and find out what it means.

squelch *v.* walk with wet sucking sound, as in walking through mud. *n.* sound that this makes.

It's in alphabetical order. Dead easy.

A Glossary explains Difficult Words

A glossary is a list of difficult words and what they mean.

If the writer thinks you won't understand something, it goes in the glossary.

A glossary is like a mini-dictionary.

A Thesaurus helps you Find Different Words

Look up a word in a thesaurus — and you'll find loads of other words that mean the same thing.

cold arctic, bitter, chilly, cool, freezing, frosty, frozen, wintry

For the last time, my name's Tyrannosaurus — not Thesaurus.

Use a thesaurus to find better words to use in your writing.

Words that mean the same thing are called synonyms (see P.17)

An Encyclopaedia is Full of Information

An encyclopaedia is full of information and pictures about all kinds of subjects.

Encyclopaedias are always in alphabetical order — so to find the capital of China you'd look up China in the C section.

C
China
Capital: Beijing
Populatio

Thesaurus — isn't that an extinct species...

The names are a bit grim, I admit, but all you need to know is how you use each one. Use a dictionary and a thesaurus to look up words as you go along — your writing will be stacks better. You can find all sorts of fascinating facts in an encyclopaedia, so go on, dive in and enjoy.

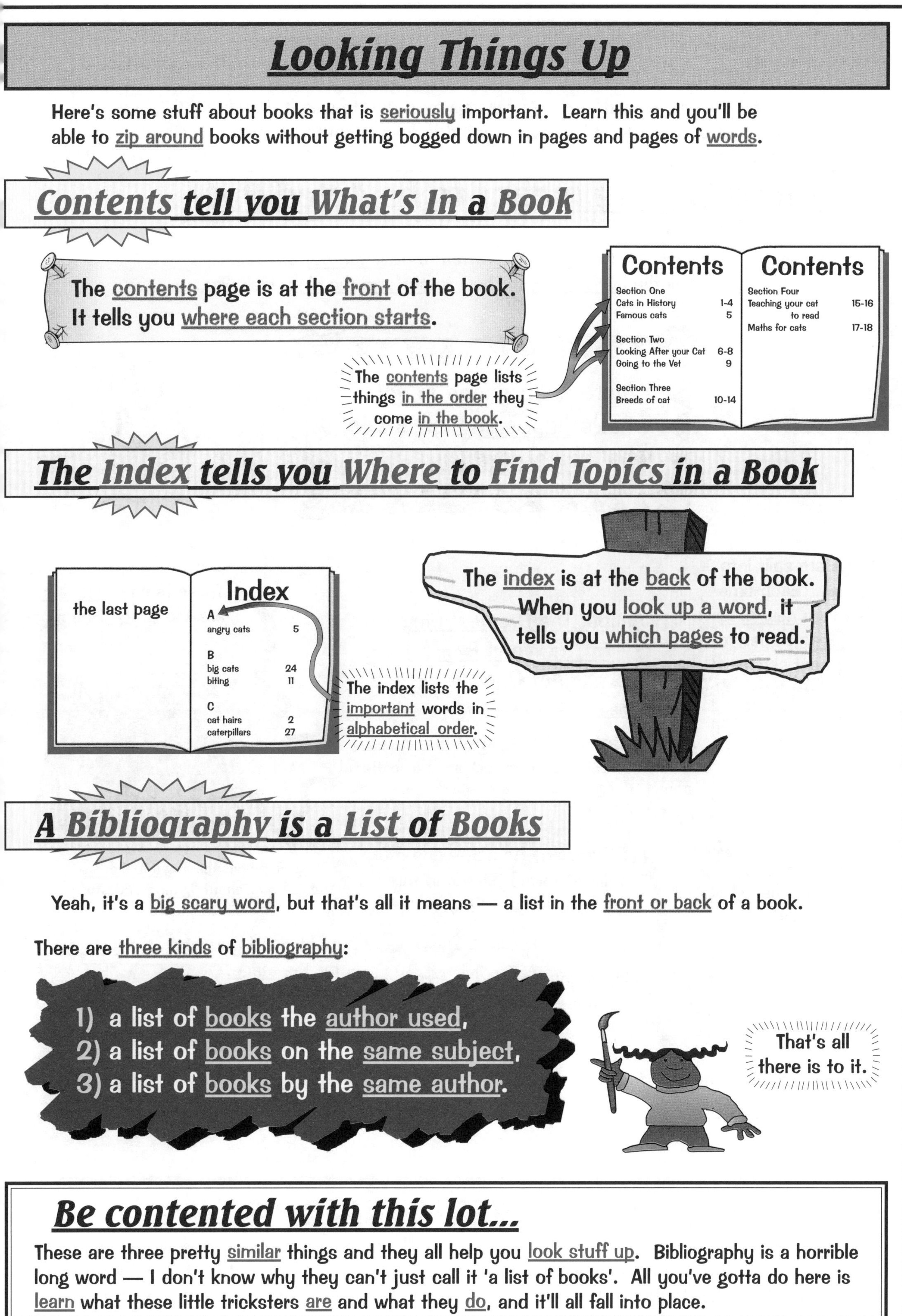

Looking Things Up

Here's some stuff about books that is seriously important. Learn this and you'll be able to zip around books without getting bogged down in pages and pages of words.

Contents tell you What's In a Book

The contents page is at the front of the book. It tells you where each section starts.

The contents page lists things in the order they come in the book.

The Index tells you Where to Find Topics in a Book

The index lists the important words in alphabetical order.

The index is at the back of the book. When you look up a word, it tells you which pages to read.

A Bibliography is a List of Books

Yeah, it's a big scary word, but that's all it means — a list in the front or back of a book.

There are three kinds of bibliography:

1) a list of books the author used,
2) a list of books on the same subject,
3) a list of books by the same author.

Be contented with this lot...

These are three pretty similar things and they all help you look stuff up. Bibliography is a horrible long word — I don't know why they can't just call it 'a list of books'. All you've gotta do here is learn what these little tricksters are and what they do, and it'll all fall into place.

Reading Plays

Plays are a bit strange to read — they're always more fun to watch, I reckon. Still, you can't get out of it. Here's everything you ever wanted to know about playscripts. Enjoy...

Playscripts are meant to be Acted Out

A playscript is the script for a play. It's written to be acted out on stage.
The playscript has all the instructions for how to perform the play, including:

- Where each scene is set,
- what's happening on stage,
- what the actors say.

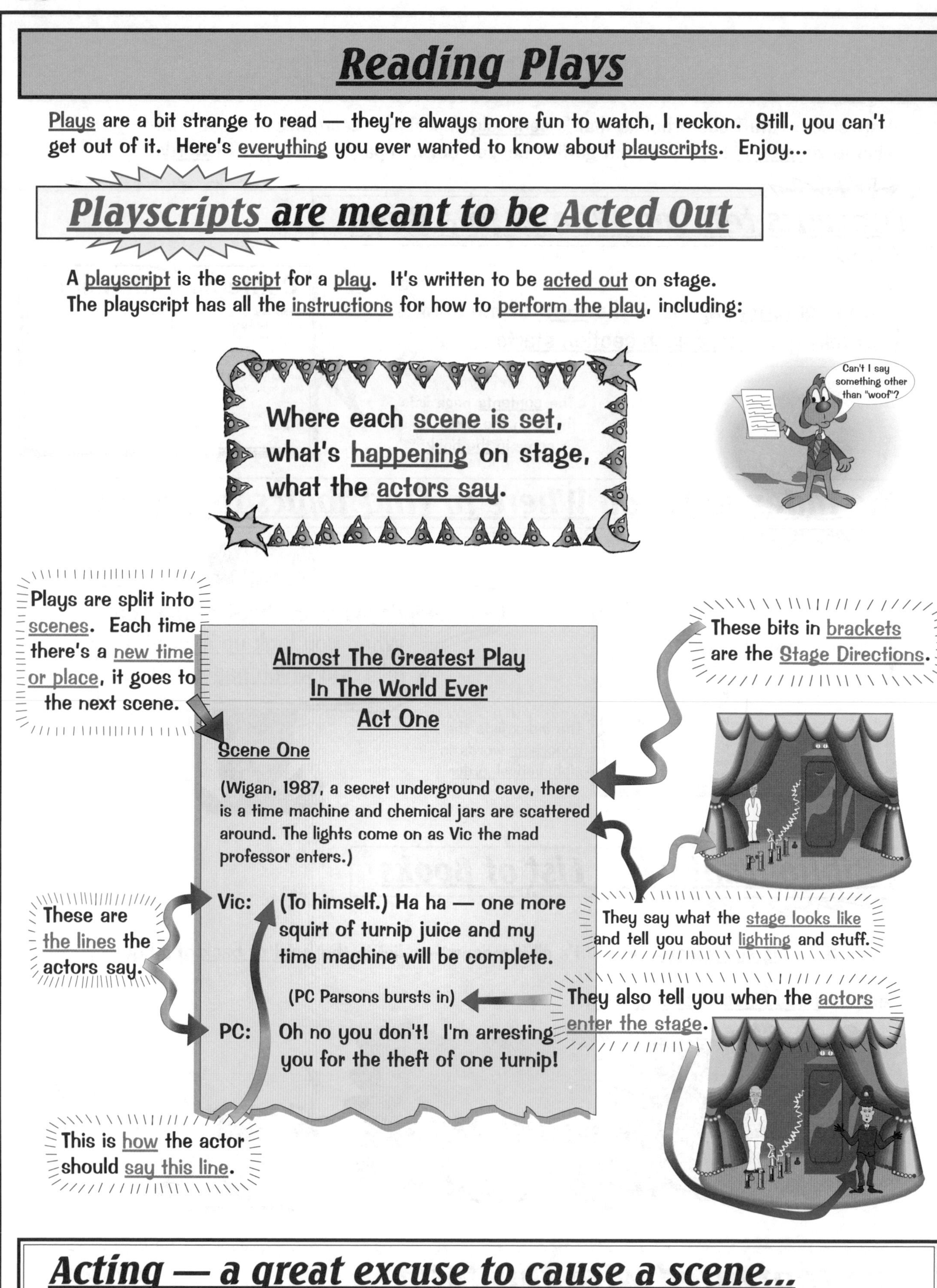

Almost The Greatest Play
In The World Ever
Act One

Scene One

(Wigan, 1987, a secret underground cave, there is a time machine and chemical jars are scattered around. The lights come on as Vic the mad professor enters.)

Vic: (To himself.) Ha ha — one more squirt of turnip juice and my time machine will be complete.

(PC Parsons bursts in)

PC: Oh no you don't! I'm arresting you for the theft of one turnip!

Acting — a great excuse to cause a scene...

Playscripts look a bit odd at first — they seem like all talk and no story. But really the actors tell the story by acting it out. Remember not to read the stage directions out loud, they're there to tell the actors what to do and how to say their lines so they can make the play believable.

Riddles and Tongue Twisters

Riddles and tongue-twisters are tops I reckon — more fun than you can poke a stick at.

A Riddle is a Clever Question

A riddle is a question that's been worded so that you can't tell straight away what it means.

What goes on four legs, then two legs, then three?
Answer my question and you will go free.
Answer it quickly or sorry you'll be.

The answer to this one is a human being.
We crawl on all fours when we're babies,
we walk on two legs as adults and
when we're old, we walk with a stick (three legs).

Tongue-twisters are Hard to Say

Tongue-twisters have got lots of similar consonant sounds, and they all get horribly mixed up when you try to say them quickly. That's why...

tongue-twisters are tricky to twist your tongue round.

This keeps repeating the sounds t, tw and tr — wouldn't want to try that with a mouthful of food...

red lorry, yellow lorry,
red lorry, yellow lorry

r l
y

th f
thr fl

That fat thrush flew
through the thorny thicket.

Tongue-tied — tired twister ties tongue to tonsils ...

I'd say you've come across these before — don't skip this bit though, you do actually need to know how they work. See if you can come up with your own riddles and tongue-twisters.

Writing a Story

Whether you're writing a story or reading one, you could do with knowing these three things.

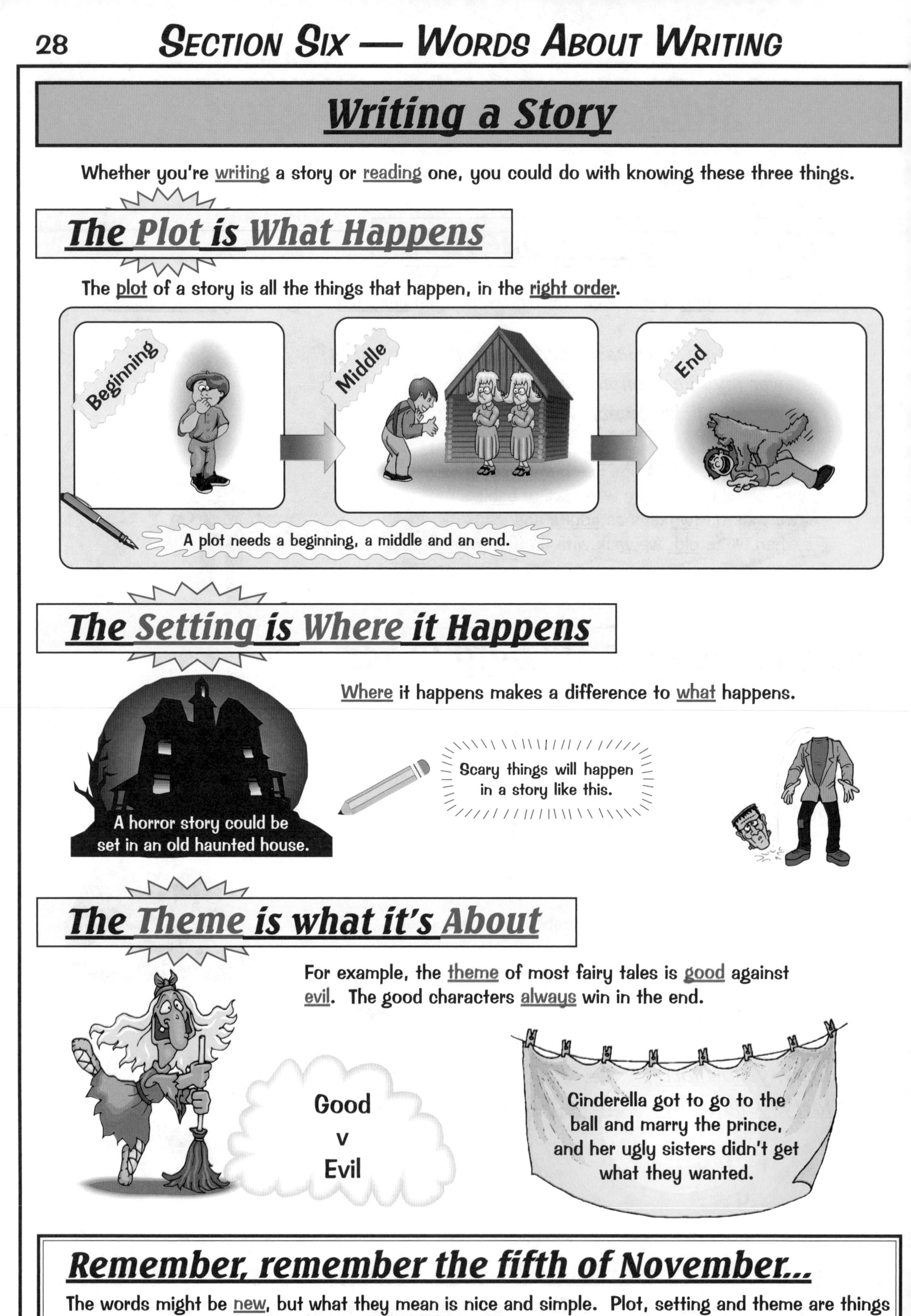

The Plot is What Happens

The plot of a story is all the things that happen, in the right order.

The Setting is Where it Happens

Where it happens makes a difference to what happens.

The Theme is what it's About

For example, the theme of most fairy tales is good against evil. The good characters always win in the end.

Remember, remember the fifth of November...

The words might be new, but what they mean is nice and simple. Plot, setting and theme are things that all stories have got. You need to spot them and say how they work — so learn them.

Telling a Story and Dialogue

Who's talking in a story is important. Here's all the juicy bits you need to know about telling a story and speaking in a story.

The Narrator is the Person Telling the Story

I carefully opened the jar and spread the jam over my head.

The narrator is in the story.

Peter and Pippa played in the snow.

The narrator isn't in the story.

Dialogue is when People Speak in a Story

Speech in a story needs speechmarks to show where it starts and stops.

Dialogue lets you know what's happening.

Question marks and exclamation marks let you know that Lucy is upset and Danielle is asking a question.

"Oh, no!" cried Lucy.
"What's up?" asked Danielle.
"The box isn't here!"said Lucy, in a panic. "It's gone!"

The characters are talking to each other about what's happening in the story.

The narrator doesn't need to say that the box had gone missing — you know that from what Danielle and Lucy have said.

Story writing — a good excuse for telling tales...

The narrator can be in the story or they can be telling the story about someone else. Dialogue is a fancy word for when people talk — it's amazing how a bit of speech helps move a story along.

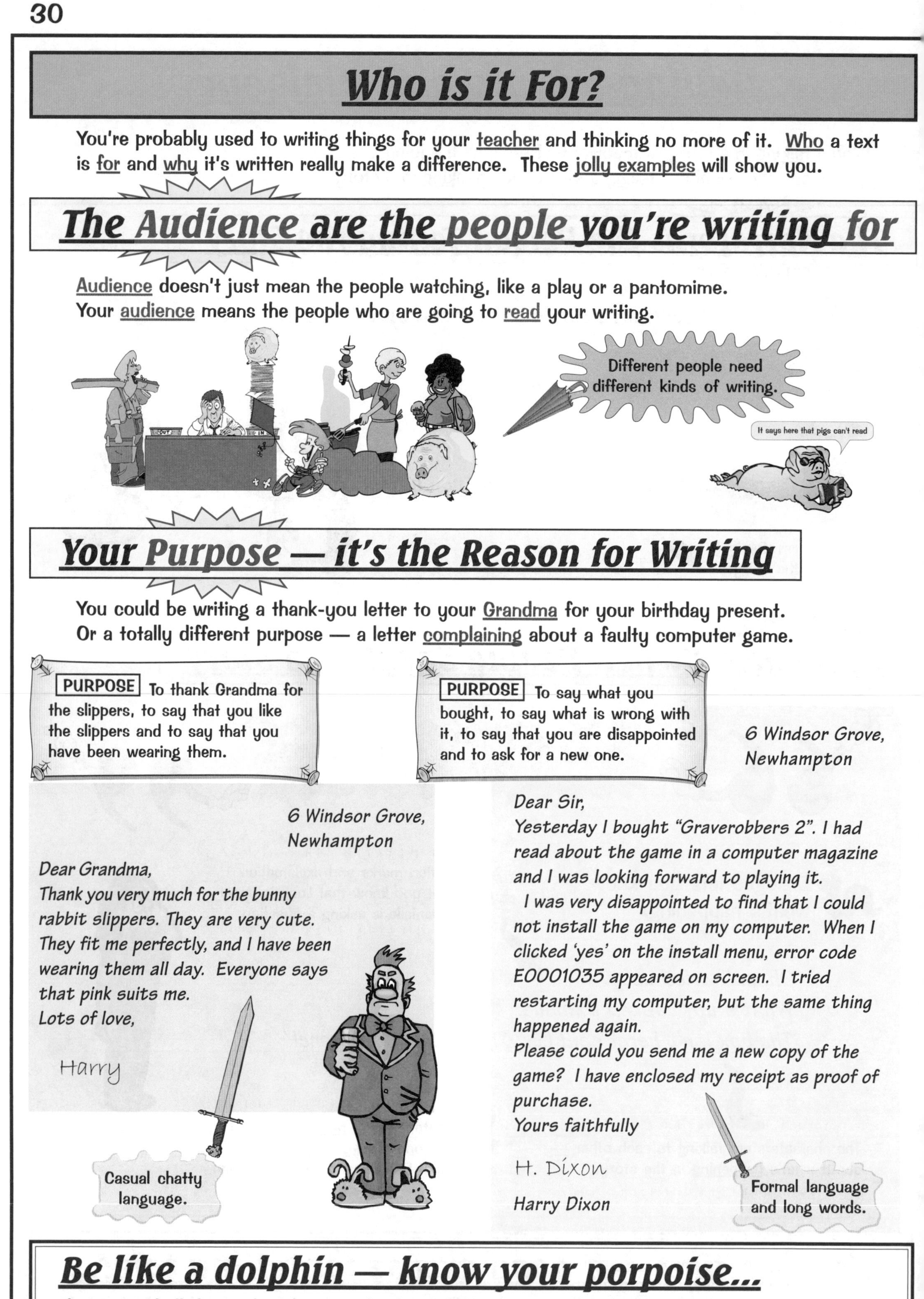

Who is it For?

You're probably used to writing things for your teacher and thinking no more of it. Who a text is for and why it's written really make a difference. These jolly examples will show you.

The Audience are the people you're writing for

Audience doesn't just mean the people watching, like a play or a pantomime.
Your audience means the people who are going to read your writing.

Your Purpose — it's the Reason for Writing

You could be writing a thank-you letter to your Grandma for your birthday present.
Or a totally different purpose — a letter complaining about a faulty computer game.

PURPOSE To thank Grandma for the slippers, to say that you like the slippers and to say that you have been wearing them.

6 Windsor Grove,
Newhampton

Dear Grandma,
Thank you very much for the bunny rabbit slippers. They are very cute. They fit me perfectly, and I have been wearing them all day. Everyone says that pink suits me.
Lots of love,

Harry

PURPOSE To say what you bought, to say what is wrong with it, to say that you are disappointed and to ask for a new one.

6 Windsor Grove,
Newhampton

Dear Sir,
Yesterday I bought "Graverobbers 2". I had read about the game in a computer magazine and I was looking forward to playing it.
I was very disappointed to find that I could not install the game on my computer. When I clicked 'yes' on the install menu, error code E0001035 appeared on screen. I tried restarting my computer, but the same thing happened again.
Please could you send me a new copy of the game? I have enclosed my receipt as proof of purchase.
Yours faithfully

H. Dixon

Harry Dixon

Be like a dolphin — know your porpoise...

The point of all this is that there are loads of different ways of writing. The way you write depends on what the writing is for and who's going to read it. Think about it, it makes sense.

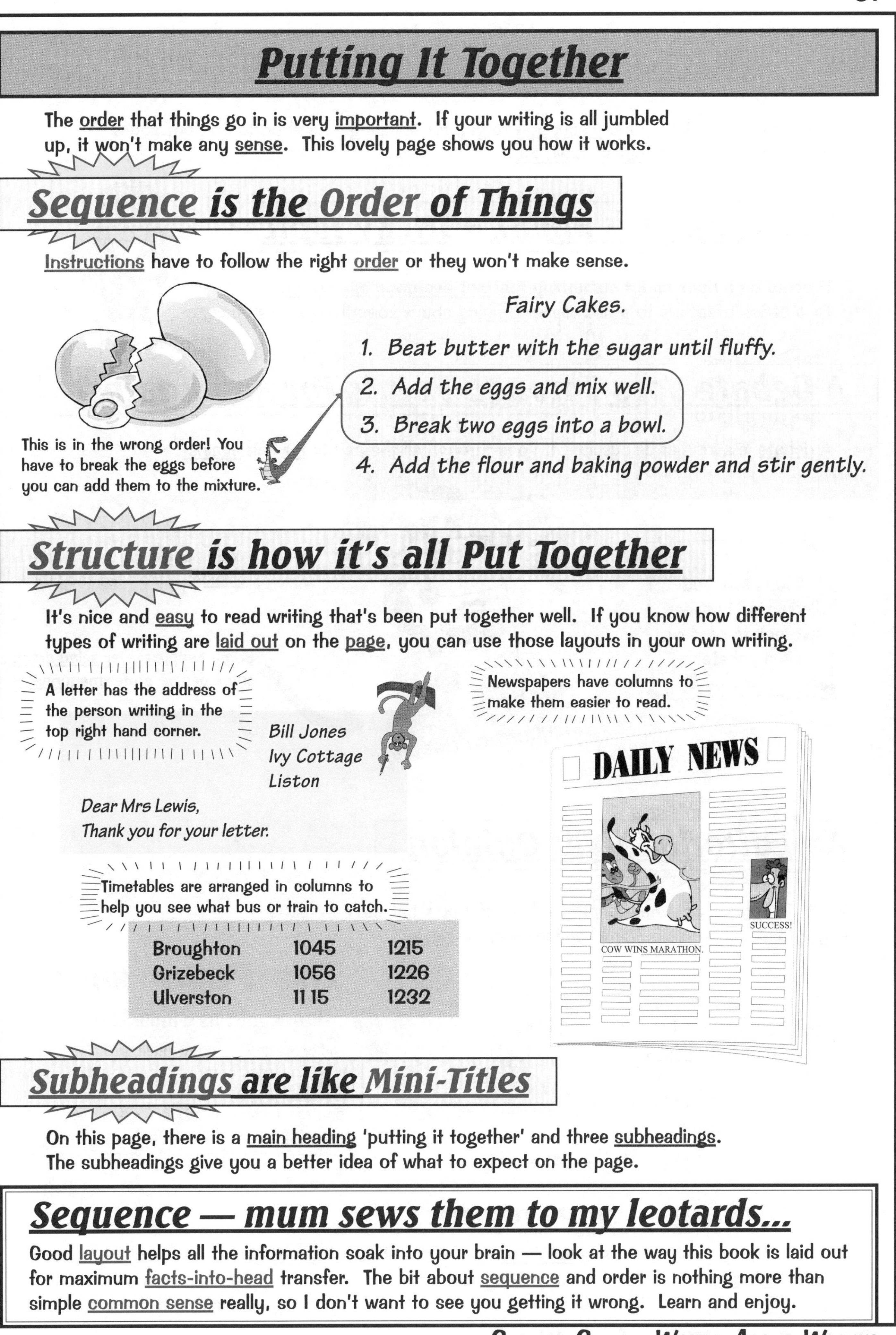

Putting It Together

The order that things go in is very important. If your writing is all jumbled up, it won't make any sense. This lovely page shows you how it works.

Sequence is the Order of Things

Instructions have to follow the right order or they won't make sense.

Fairy Cakes.

1. *Beat butter with the sugar until fluffy.*
2. *Add the eggs and mix well.*
3. *Break two eggs into a bowl.*
4. *Add the flour and baking powder and stir gently.*

This is in the wrong order! You have to break the eggs before you can add them to the mixture.

Structure is how it's all Put Together

It's nice and easy to read writing that's been put together well. If you know how different types of writing are laid out on the page, you can use those layouts in your own writing.

A letter has the address of the person writing in the top right hand corner.

Bill Jones
Ivy Cottage
Liston

Dear Mrs Lewis,
Thank you for your letter.

Newspapers have columns to make them easier to read.

Timetables are arranged in columns to help you see what bus or train to catch.

Broughton	1045	1215
Grizebeck	1056	1226
Ulverston	11 15	1232

Subheadings are like Mini-Titles

On this page, there is a main heading 'putting it together' and three subheadings. The subheadings give you a better idea of what to expect on the page.

Sequence — mum sews them to my leotards...

Good layout helps all the information soak into your brain — look at the way this book is laid out for maximum facts-into-head transfer. The bit about sequence and order is nothing more than simple common sense really, so I don't want to see you getting it wrong. Learn and enjoy.

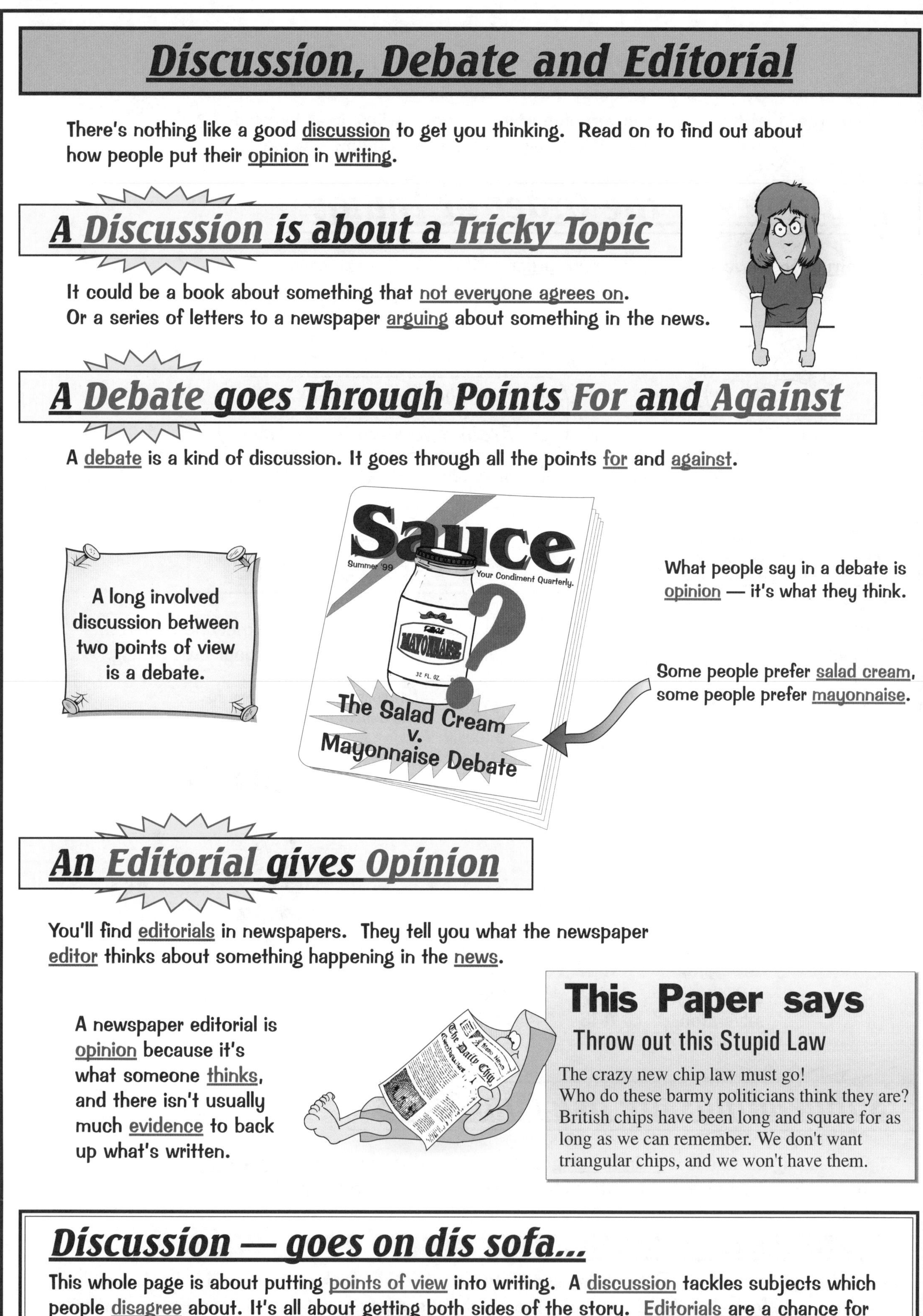

Discussion, Debate and Editorial

There's nothing like a good discussion to get you thinking. Read on to find out about how people put their opinion in writing.

A Discussion is about a Tricky Topic

It could be a book about something that not everyone agrees on.
Or a series of letters to a newspaper arguing about something in the news.

A Debate goes Through Points For and Against

A debate is a kind of discussion. It goes through all the points for and against.

A long involved discussion between two points of view is a debate.

What people say in a debate is opinion — it's what they think.

Some people prefer salad cream, some people prefer mayonnaise.

An Editorial gives Opinion

You'll find editorials in newspapers. They tell you what the newspaper editor thinks about something happening in the news.

A newspaper editorial is opinion because it's what someone thinks, and there isn't usually much evidence to back up what's written.

This Paper says

Throw out this Stupid Law

The crazy new chip law must go!
Who do these barmy politicians think they are? British chips have been long and square for as long as we can remember. We don't want triangular chips, and we won't have them.

Discussion — goes on dis sofa...

This whole page is about putting points of view into writing. A discussion tackles subjects which people disagree about. It's all about getting both sides of the story. Editorials are a chance for newspapers to speak out — if you don't agree you can always wrap your chips in them.

Persuasive Writing

Have you ever been sure that you're right and nobody else believed you?
Well, this is what this page is all about, making people believe what you say.

Persuasive writing gives a Point of View

Writing that tries to persuade people of a point of view is called persuasive writing, which seems fairly obvious.

Work out what you want to say as a list of points.
Here's an example about school uniform.

1) School uniform is outdated.

2) You can't be individual in school uniform.

3) People should be allowed to wear what they like.

4) School uniform isn't necessary.

Get them into the right order, so they kind of follow on from each other.

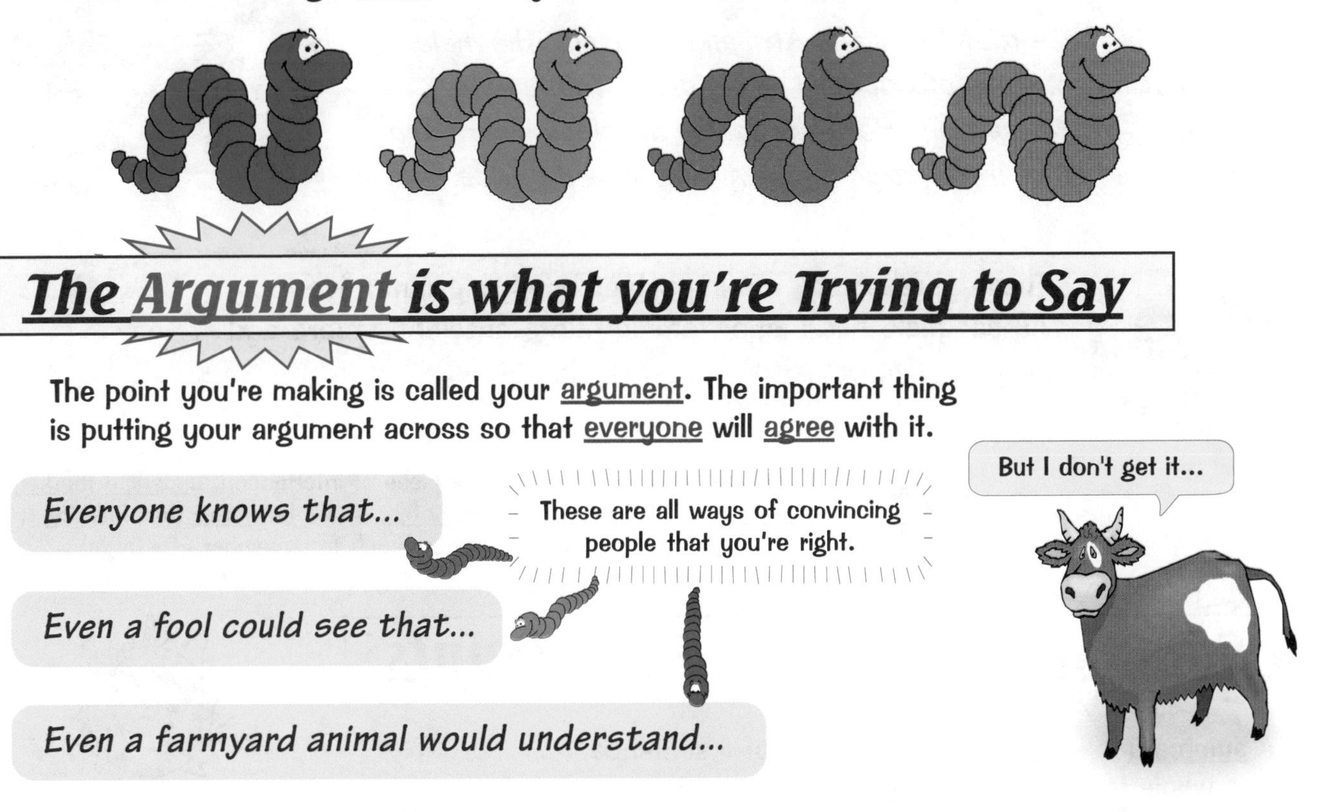

The Argument is what you're Trying to Say

The point you're making is called your argument. The important thing is putting your argument across so that everyone will agree with it.

Everyone knows that...

Even a fool could see that...

Even a farmyard animal would understand...

I'm always right — why won't you admit it?

Important stuff this — there's nothing worse than people not believing a word you say. Even if you're sure about your argument, you still need good writing skills to make other people agree with you. An argument doesn't mean a fight here, it's all the points you're trying to make.

Key Words — Important Phrases

You'll have to agree — it's much easier to remember key points than a whole lot of words.

Key Words are the Most Important

The key words in a sentence or a paragraph give you the real nitty-gritty of the meaning. The other words add a few frills and detail, but aren't absolutely essential. Here's an example from a newspaper article to show how it works.

Warm-hearted Salworth schoolchildren have raised over £2000 for the Kosovan refugee appeal by holding a series of coffee mornings in the school hall.

You can pick out 'schoolchildren', '£2000', 'refugee appeal' and 'coffee mornings' here

Key Phrases are the Most Important

You don't need to remember every single word of a bit of writing to remember what it was about. Key phrases tell you what it's getting at.

Lions are big cats that live in the African savannah. The male has a distinctive mane of thick fur on his neck. The female does most of the hunting. Her prey can be antelope, zebra and wildebeeste. Lions live in large family groups called prides.

These phrases are the important ones: big cats; live in Africa; male has mane; female hunts antelope, zebra and wildebeeste; group of lions called a pride.

If you really want to remember a piece of information, underline the key phrases and write them down as notes. It's a lot better than learning it off by heart, because there's not so much to remember. Or forget...

A Summary has all the Main Points

A summary is a shortened-down form of a sentence or a whole text. All the important points are there, so you get the general idea of what's been said.

no, not summery...

Chubb — they know all about keys...

Nobody could expect you to remember something word for word. If you write the main points as notes it helps you to understand what it's all about — and it helps you to remember it, too.

Skim Reading and Scanning

This page will save you a lot of time and effort. You don't always have to read every little thing in detail — which is a good thing if you ask me.

Skimming is Reading for a Rough Picture

Skim reading gives a rough idea of what a text is about. It's like looking at something quickly and having a blurred picture of it in your head. Look at it carefully, and you get more detail.

Scanning is Reading for Key Words

When you want to find something in an index, it's much quicker to let your eyes wander over the page on the lookout for the word you want.

I scanned the barcode on the skimmed milk...

Finally, something you'll be happy to learn — you don't always have to read every little detail. Sometimes all you need to do is skim read to get the important bits. If you're looking for a particular subject just scan through until you find the word you are after. It all saves time.

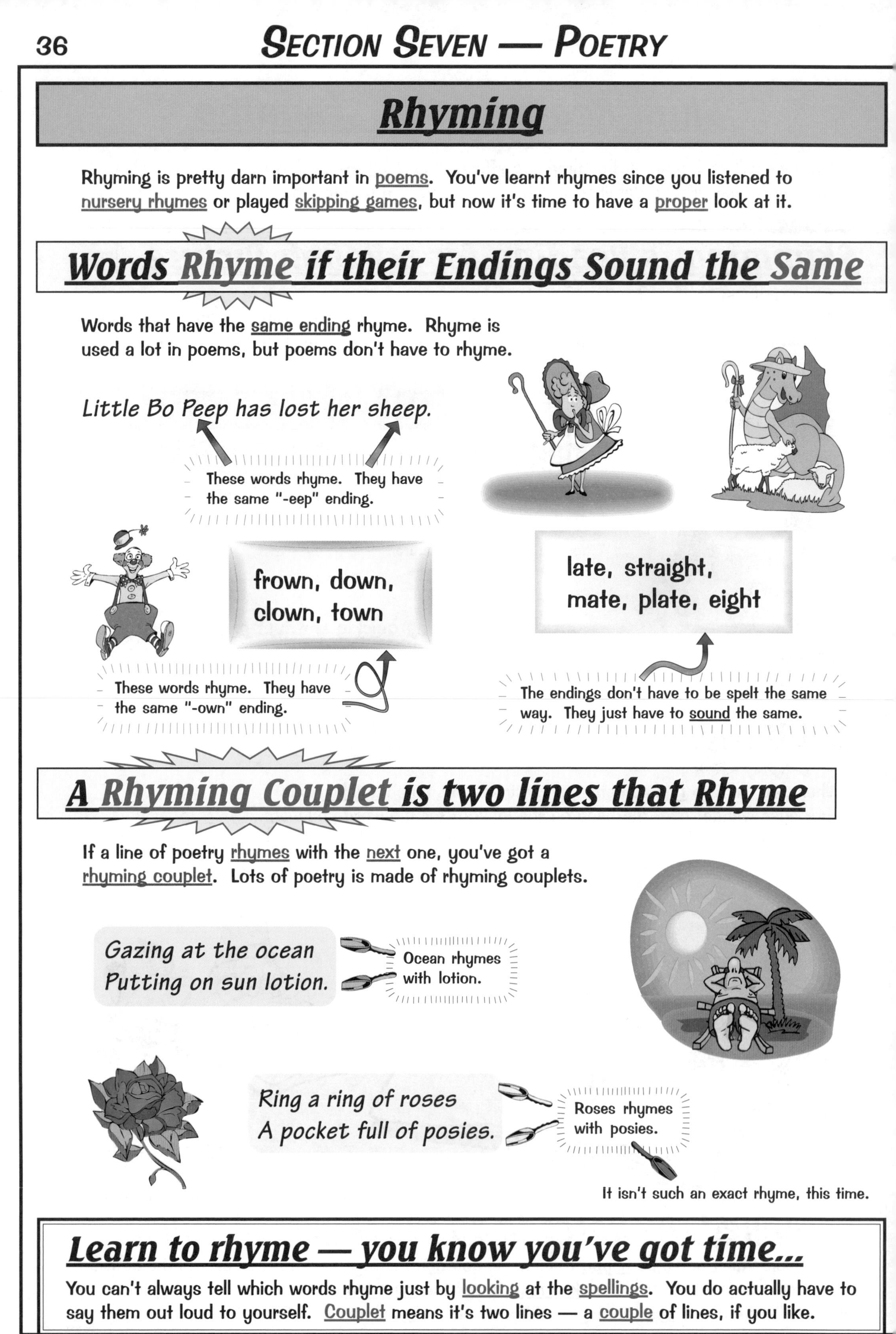

Rhyming

Rhyming is pretty darn important in poems. You've learnt rhymes since you listened to nursery rhymes or played skipping games, but now it's time to have a proper look at it.

Words Rhyme if their Endings Sound the Same

Words that have the same ending rhyme. Rhyme is used a lot in poems, but poems don't have to rhyme.

Little Bo Peep has lost her sheep.

These words rhyme. They have the same "-eep" ending.

frown, down, clown, town

These words rhyme. They have the same "-own" ending.

late, straight, mate, plate, eight

The endings don't have to be spelt the same way. They just have to sound the same.

A Rhyming Couplet is two lines that Rhyme

If a line of poetry rhymes with the next one, you've got a rhyming couplet. Lots of poetry is made of rhyming couplets.

Gazing at the ocean
Putting on sun lotion.

Ocean rhymes with lotion.

Ring a ring of roses
A pocket full of posies.

Roses rhymes with posies.

It isn't such an exact rhyme, this time.

Learn to rhyme — you know you've got time...

You can't always tell which words rhyme just by looking at the spellings. You do actually have to say them out loud to yourself. Couplet means it's two lines — a couple of lines, if you like.

Verse, Chorus and Stanza

It's easy to remember that poems and songs are divided up into verses and choruses, but now you've got a posh new word to learn, too. "Stanza" — it sounds Italian...

A Verse is a Section of a Poem

A group of lines in a poem or a song is called a verse.
The verses in a poem have different words, but they follow the same pattern.

Verse 1) She'll be coming round the mountain when she comes,
She'll be coming round the mountain when she comes.
She'll be coming round the mountain,
Coming round the mountain,
Coming round the mountain when she comes.

chorus: Singing aye, aye, yippee, yippee aye, etc

Verse 2) She'll be wearing pink pyjamas when she comes,
She'll be wearing pink pyjamas when she comes...

A Chorus goes Between the Verses in a Poem

The verses in a song or a poem are different.
The chorus is always the same, and it goes between all the verses.

This is the chorus. It goes between the verses in the song and it always stays the same.

Singing aye, aye, yippee, yippee aye.
Singing aye, aye, yippee, yippee aye.
Singing aye, aye, yippee,
aye, aye, yippee,
aye, aye, yippee, yippee aye.

You get the idea...

Stanza is another word for Verse

A stanza is a group of lines in a poem. The pattern of syllables and rhyming is the same for all the stanzas in the poem.

Everyone join in with the chorus...

You'd think they'd be happy calling a verse a verse and a chorus a chorus, but no, they have to throw in this word "stanza". Don't worry about it, it's just another word for a verse in a poem.

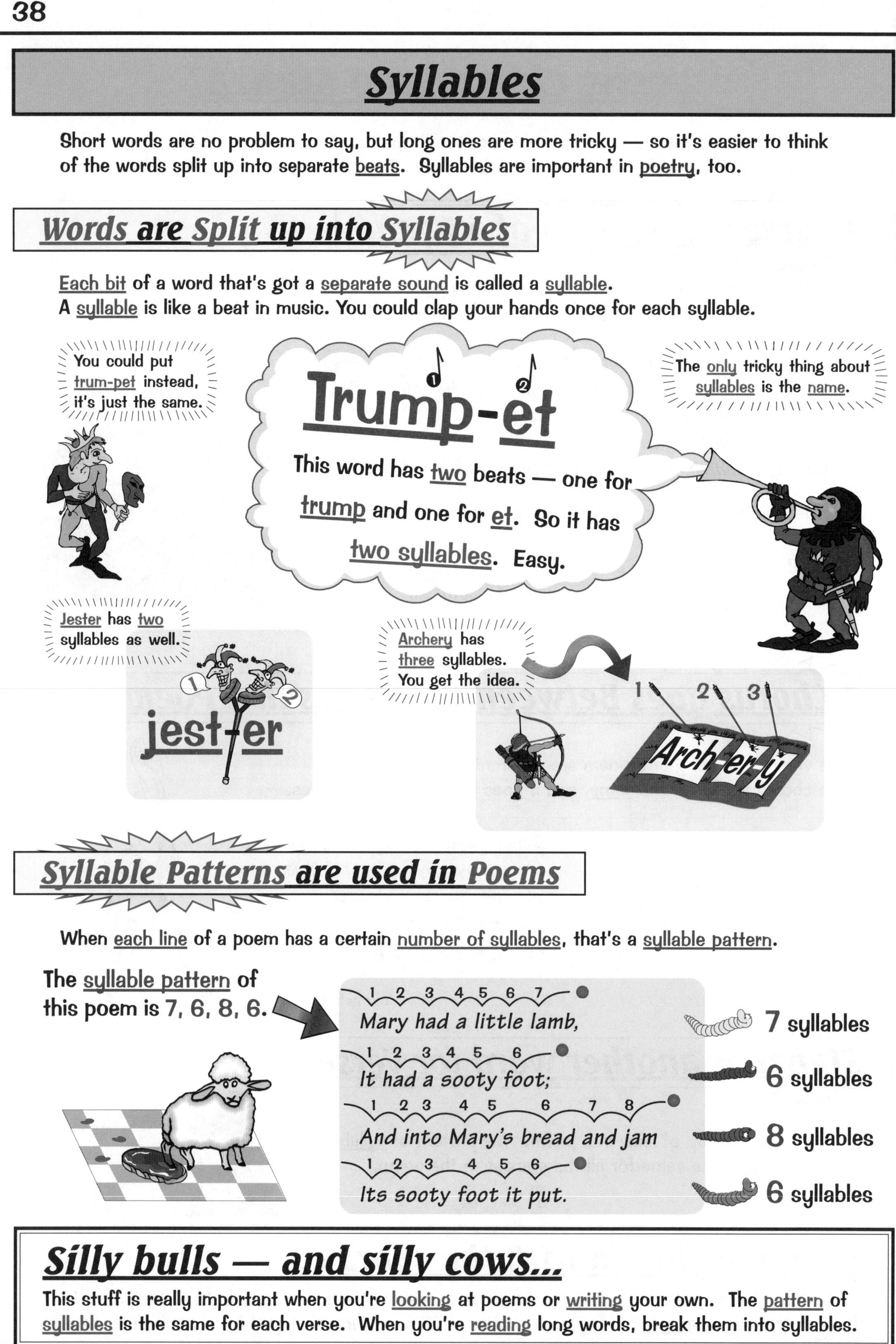

Syllables

Short words are no problem to say, but long ones are more tricky — so it's easier to think of the words split up into separate beats. Syllables are important in poetry, too.

Words are Split up into Syllables

Each bit of a word that's got a separate sound is called a syllable.
A syllable is like a beat in music. You could clap your hands once for each syllable.

Syllable Patterns are used in Poems

When each line of a poem has a certain number of syllables, that's a syllable pattern.

The syllable pattern of this poem is 7, 6, 8, 6.

Silly bulls — and silly cows...

This stuff is really important when you're looking at poems or writing your own. The pattern of syllables is the same for each verse. When you're reading long words, break them into syllables.

Cinquains and Haiku

Don't worry, these funny looking words are just names for two more types of poem. The big thing about both of them is the number of syllables that they've got to have.

Cinquains have a 22 Syllable Pattern

Cinquains are poems which always have the same pattern of syllables. They have five lines which don't rhyme and have 22 syllables altogether. The syllables are in a 2,4,6,8,2, pattern.

	Number of syllables
Summer:	2
Sun shines so hot.	4
Cat stretches in the heat,	6
Dog lies down under cool tree shade,	8
To sleep.	2

five lines

The Haiku is a Japanese type of Poem

Haiku are short poems with seventeen syllables. They only have three lines and their syllables always follow a 5,7,5 pattern like this:

	Number of syllables
Small blushing flowers	5
Float softly down from the trees;	7
Cherry blossom time.	5

three lines

Haiku are nice and easy to write, because they're so short and they don't have to rhyme.

Haiku — bless you! Have a tissue...

These poems don't have to rhyme. The number of syllables in each line is what's important. Remember how many lines each kind of poem must have: cinquains have 5; haiku have 3.

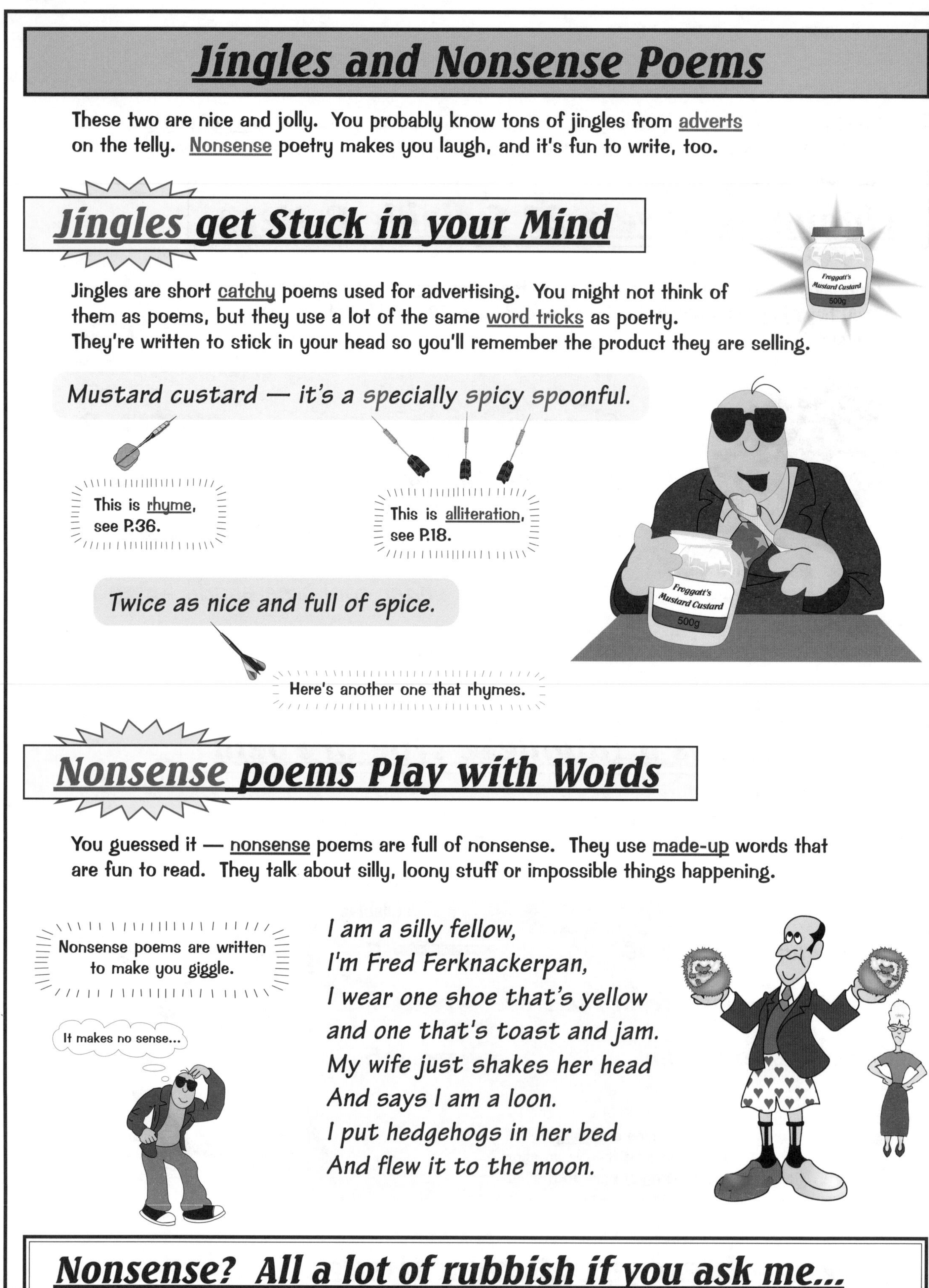

Jingles and Nonsense Poems

These two are nice and jolly. You probably know tons of jingles from adverts on the telly. Nonsense poetry makes you laugh, and it's fun to write, too.

Jingles get Stuck in your Mind

Jingles are short catchy poems used for advertising. You might not think of them as poems, but they use a lot of the same word tricks as poetry. They're written to stick in your head so you'll remember the product they are selling.

Mustard custard — it's a specially spicy spoonful.

This is rhyme, see P.36.

This is alliteration, see P.18.

Twice as nice and full of spice.

Here's another one that rhymes.

Nonsense poems Play with Words

You guessed it — nonsense poems are full of nonsense. They use made-up words that are fun to read. They talk about silly, loony stuff or impossible things happening.

Nonsense poems are written to make you giggle.

It makes no sense...

I am a silly fellow,
I'm Fred Ferknackerpan,
I wear one shoe that's yellow
and one that's toast and jam.
My wife just shakes her head
And says I am a loon.
I put hedgehogs in her bed
And flew it to the moon.

Nonsense? All a lot of rubbish if you ask me...

You don't need to know why a jingle's called a jingle. All you need to bother yourself with is what one is and what it's for. Nonsense poems are good clean fun, and well worth knowing about.

Calligrams and Shape Poems

Calligrams and shape poems aren't your run-of-the-mill everyday poems, that's for sure. They have added extras which make them eye-catching and fun.

Calligrams have Fancy Writing

Calligrams are poems that are written in fancy letters that have something to do with what the poem's about. You can really use your imagination here and come up with some hot letters, cold letters, fat letters, thin letters, scary letters...

On a cold, frosty morning,
My window is glazed with ice
In zigzag patterns like an Indian blanket.
Outside, leaves have thick white edges:
Spiders' webs are diamond jewelled.

This is written in frosty letters.

The pattern behind the words looks like ice.

Shape Poems are Written in a Special Shape

The words in a shape poem are written into a shape that has something to do with what the poem's about.

It's about spiders, so it's written in a web — groovy.

Lucy spied a spider, lurking in her cider. With a frown, she drank it down, And now it lives inside her.

It's about pyramids, so it's written in the shape of one.

In
Egpyt
Pharaohs
Built pyramids:
Palaces to be buried in.

Shape poems — Ode to a Triangle...

It's got to be said — good presentation really makes a huge difference. These two kinds of poetry really grab your eye — they're not just words thrown down on the page any old how.

Index

Index

Index